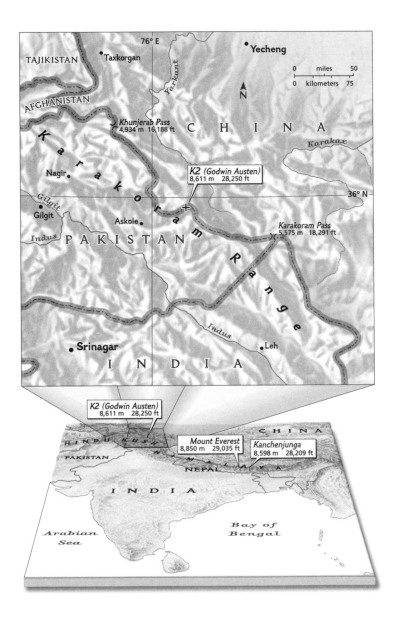

K2

ONE WOMAN'S QUEST FOR THE SUMMIT

K2

ONE WOMAN'S QUEST FOR THE SUMMIT

Heidi Howkins

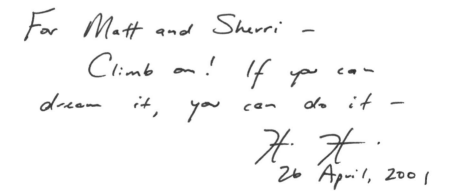

For Matt and Sherri —
Climb on! If you can
dream it, you can do it —
H. H.
26 April, 2001

ADVENTURE PRESS

NATIONAL GEOGRAPHIC
WASHINGTON, D. C.

Library of Congress Cataloging-in-Publication Data

Howkins, Heidi.
  K2 : one woman's quest for the summit / Heidi Howkins.
    p. cm,
  ISBN 0-7922-7996-4
    1. Howkins, Heidi. 2. Women mountaineers--United States--Biography. 3.
Mountaineers--United States--Biography. 4, Mountaineering--Himalaya Mountains. I.
Title.

GV 199.92.H69 A3 2001
796.52'2'092--dc21
[B]

                                                          2001030265

Printed and bound by R. R. Donnelley & Sons, Crawfordsville, Indiana

Interior design by Melissa Farris and Suez Kehl Corrado

For Devi, my complicated daughter,
and for Bill, who is not afraid
of complicated women

CONTENTS

PROLOGUE

It wasn't the first time I had felt that choking sensation, the panicky feeling of not having enough air. We were at 25,000 feet on the north side of K2, the "savage mountain," and our tent had just been crushed by a wet wave of falling snow. The fabric was torn, the poles were broken, and I was flailing in the chaos trying to push up with my back to create a pocket of space underneath me. I was trying to remember where I had put my boots and was shouting to our teammates in the other tent.

Up until that moment, it had been an ordinary day of climbing. The five of us—four climbers on the "K2000" expedition and a cameraman—had spent four hours climbing up to Camp 3, another hour or two hacking a small platform into the steep snow-and-rock slope, and another hour or two melting snow to rehydrate ourselves. After that, we snuggled into the smooth nylon warmth of our sleeping bags. The weather was disintegrating, spitting snow crystals at the walls of our tent, but I refused to let my thoughts linger on the possibility that we would again have to descend because of bad weather. Instead I focused on the climb ahead: the labyrinth of broken cliffs just above us and the final slopes leading to the summit.

And then, suddenly, we were entombed.

THE NORTHWEST RIDGE OF K2 WAS MY FIFTH HIMALAYAN expedition in five years. Five of the most challenging climbs in the world: Gasherbrum II; the north face of Kanchenjunga; the notorious south side of K2; Everest, without supplemental oxygen; and the remote north side of K2, again. Five years of experimenting with different climbing styles and expedition techniques, sometimes solo, sometimes with two or three partners, sometimes with larger groups, endeavoring always to climb in a "minimalist" style, without supplemental oxygen or the assistance of high-altitude porters.

Five years of storms and avalanches.

Five years of learning the art of remote motherhood, of communicating via satellite phone and e-mail with my daughter, halfway around the world. (Can I get my ears pierced, Mom? I lost a tooth, Mom!)

Five years of triumph over fear and anger, of learning to deal with the fact that I am a woman in a male-dominated climbing world.

Oh, to be a member of the fraternity, the brotherhood of the rope! My journey over these past five years would have been so different. I was the only female climber on each team, in most cases the only woman on the mountain. Sometimes more, sometimes less of a woman; as a woman in a world of male climbers, you have to either lose or use your femininity to stabilize the gender tensions.

But I'm getting ahead of myself here.

FROM WITHIN THE ENVELOPE OF SNOW, WE MANAGED TO find the ice-encrusted zipper at one end of the tent. My tentmate, cameraman Greg Ritchie, tunneled his way out of the door. Through the slit I could just see his bare hands, scraping the snow out of his boots.

And then another spray of heavy snow broke over the cliff above and came hissing down.

I held the flap of the tent closed tightly and braced myself for the worst. Would the whole slope let loose? My hands blindly wormed into the crushed corners of the tent, groping for Greg's gloves and my boots. I heard the shovel and a voice outside.

My fingers suddenly felt the contours of a metal object with Greg's gloves right under it. I gently extricated them from the mess and squirmed back through the snow that was spilling in through the open crack.

"Greg! Here!" the effort had left me breathless, "I've got the camera, too."

"You found the camera? Good, thanks. Pass it out." As I passed the gloves through the hole, I could see the tension in his furrowed brow.

Real epiphanies come in small moments.

Reading between the lines in his forehead, I could see that we were in danger of being swept off the mountain by another wave of snow.

Normally, getting buried alive during a casual afternoon nap would be the kind of thing that would haunt me in my worst nightmares—the suffocating, silently screaming kind of dreams where you wake with your mouth and nose buried in the sheets.

But after getting buried in an avalanche in 1997, and digging out the bodies of two men after an avalanche in 1998, the concept of killer waves of snow had somehow become a part of a day's work.

My fear was gone.

Which, if you accept the traditional wisdom of the sport, would mean that it was time to go home—fear is the tool that keeps climbers alive.

STANDING OUTSIDE THE CRUSHED TENT, SHIVERING WITH wet clothes pressed against our skin, Greg and I looked at each other, each silently assessing the odds, the risks, the options. It was still snowing. We couldn't see the slope above the cliffs, and we didn't know whether it was loaded, whether the entire slope might let go and sweep us to the glacier 5,000 feet below.

"We still have that tent we carried up for Camp 4," I pointed out.

We might be able to dig another little ledge for it. If we could hack through the ice and rocks just under the snow below the cliff, we might be more sheltered from the falling waves of snow.

We hesitated. It was still snowing, with no sign of a break. Should we stay, or should we go back down to Base Camp and hope for another chance at the summit?

"DO NOT," AN ADVENTURE WRITER ONCE WARNED ME, "EVER make the mistake of trying to write about why you climb." Trying to explain why anyone would sacrifice three months with family, friends, and the luxury of toilets for an opportunity to suffer and possibly die on some remote and snowy peak is like, well, like trying to explain the unexplainable. You just can't do it.

Of course, people try to write about the "why" anyway. A skydiver friend of mine recently e-mailed me a beautiful example of such an attempt. "We, as adventurers," he wrote, "have conquered our basic fears, performed under pressure, embraced life and survival with gusto. We are validating ourselves, measuring ourselves not against a relative scale of skill or merit, but against the absolutes of gravity and our own fragile existence."

Conquering fear. Embracing survival with gusto. Fragile existence. Wow, I thought, he's got it. I'll have to memorize this one for the next slide show.

But what about the flashes of light that you can see when you're up above 24,000 feet, looking down through the Earth's atmosphere? What about learning to swear in nine different languages at Base Camp? What about the agony of losing fingers or toes or a partner at a high-altitude camp? What about sitting in the snow listening to porters wailing Urdu songs about brave lovesick men?

Answering the "why climb" question is easy; there are as many reasons as there are moments.

The difficult question is "why climb to the summit?"

What is there on the summit of K2, that would entice a climber to risk everything? There is no buried treasure, no Holy

Grail, no gold trophy. It's not the highest mountain. There are the hallucinations and mystical moments, but you don't have to go to the summit for that and I wouldn't risk dying to be the first American woman to the summit. There is the warm glow of achievement, of triumph over mind and body, but this doesn't explain the impulse either.

It's something much simpler, really.

When you get to the top of K2, there's nowhere left to go. You've succeeded against the world's toughest mountain. There is the cessation of passion, of the desire to move forever upwards. There is emptiness, and the closure of a circle. You are back where you started. And you're at peace.

WE DECIDED TO STAY.

As Greg and one of our teammates started to hack at the rock and ice with their axes, I sifted through the remains of our tent, carefully salvaging and packaging each piece of equipment. We would need everything, except possibly the broken tent poles and the toothbrush with a sawed-off handle, to reach the summit.

WRITING ABOUT CLIMBING IN THE HIMALAYA IS ONE thing, producing an accurate image of the experience is another.

Piecing together this account has been a little like looking at the reflection of the moon in water. The image in my mind's eye—the image that has been painted on these pages—is clear, but somehow it doesn't seem to completely capture the real thing.

In the end, the story that has emerged here is an account of an intensely personal journey. This is only one climber's story—

one of the many climber's stories that diverged and coalesced on five Himalayan expeditions over a five year period.

It is a story about a loneliness, about flashes of lightning, about choking and learning to breathe again. About a contest, one woman versus the rock and ice and her own foibles, struggling to play the game with integrity, sometimes succeeding, sometimes failing. About experiences that left me with a lasting, aching need to climb, to struggle forever upward.

H.H.

PART ONE

the voice in my head says

love is the distance between you and what you love
whether you love what you love
or live in divided ceaseless revolt against it

what you love is your fate.

—Frank Bidart

DLA WANDA

There was something almost sinister about the print, something familiar lurking in the inky void at the edges. I didn't mean to stare at it for so long, but I couldn't help myself. The silhouette of a lone tree was framed by a luminous moon and the silky form of a woman was sitting at the base of the tree, naked except for a slender yellow collar. There was a tiger, too, lying at the woman's feet with a docile expression in its eyes, muzzle closed on what appeared to be the end of a leash.

"*Dla Wanda,*" somebody had written in neat little block letters on the back. I had been standing in the back of a used bookstore in Kathmandu, flipping through photos in mountaineering books, when it appeared at my feet. The bookstore had been doing business by candlelight for several hours, and I was hunkered down in the corner of the store with my headlamp like a hermit in a Cimmerian cave. I wasn't really looking for anything in particular, just seeking refuge from the tumult of the dark streets. From outside came the muffled sounds of the familiar chaos—a pack of wild dogs scuffling in the narrow alley outside the shop, cars swinging the orbs of their headlights around a corner down the street, hooting as they blundered into an oncoming stream of pedestrians and rickshaws.

It might have been just another evening in Kathmandu.

It *could* have been another routine premonsoon power outage.

But I'm sure it was something different. As I was reading, my headlamp began to flicker, as if an invisible moth was flitting back and forth through the beam. The air began to get thicker, as if the dust and shadows were gathering around me. And then the print appeared at my feet.

It must have been wedged between the pages of Cherie Bremer-Kamp's book *Living on the Edge* before it fell to the floor. I instinctively picked it up and examined it in the dim circle of my headlamp. I knew it was meant for me. No one in the store would have known where it came from. And, I figured, with a furtive glance at the proprietor, they certainly wouldn't know where it went. I guess you might say I stole it.

The picture didn't surface again until I was rummaging through a duffel bag full of old expedition equipment a few months ago. The duffel bag contained a boot, and the boot contained an old hat. I looked at the hat for a stupefied moment, and then stuffed it back in the boot.

THE HAT WAS NOT MINE. IT BELONGED TO MY CLIMBING partner, Iñaki who had been with me on three expeditions. I should have sent it back to him, but when he decided to climb alone on Everest in 1999, I felt deserted, betrayed, even though I knew his decision had nothing to do with our friendship. Somehow both keeping it and sending it seemed wrong, so I did the simplest wrong thing to do and kept it.

"You don't trust me," he had said before he left Base Camp, the accusation tinged with a mocking kind of sadness.

"Trust doesn't have anything to do with it," I retorted. "The problem is you've morphed into someone I can't even communicate with."

Privately, I realized he had found a way out of what I call "the labyrinth."

TWO YEARS AGO, I WAS STUCK IN A CAR FOR EIGHT HOURS with a hitchhiker from Canada. I told him the whole story of Iñaki, and my ex-husband Zee, and the labyrinth in the mountains, and as I did, I realized that the same spirit filled both my story and the image on the postcard that fell out of that book in Kathmandu—a feeling that was both familiar and uncomfortable, like a force that lures us to our fate.

The White Rabbit put on his spectacles.
"Where shall I begin, please your Majesty?"
he asked. "Begin at the beginning," the King
said, very gravely, "and go on till you come to
the end; then stop."

—LEWIS CARROLL,
Alice in Wonderland

POSTMORTEM UNDERWEAR ACQUISITION

I spotted the hitchhiker on an interstate just south of the Canadian border, a couple of hours after the first star had risen.

Highways scare me. There's something unnatural about hurtling your body through space at speeds greater than a cheetah can run. When I saw him standing in the narrow margin of the road inches away from making a mess on someone's windshield, I impulsively decided to pull over.

"New York," he replied through the half-open door in response to the obvious question. He was tall and thin, with a slight slouch. It had just started to snow, and his hair and shoulders were festooned with big fluffy flakes. That was about all I could see, but it didn't really matter. I had already decided to pick him up.

"I can take you to the state border," I offered, hoping he wouldn't ask which state border.

"Yeah, that'd be good." He swung his pack into the back seat and folded his lanky frame into the front. "Name's Hiddle."

I have observed that long distance hitchhikers have perfected the art of talking to themselves, and Hiddle was no exception. As we drove down the highway, I realized that he was still sunk in whatever interior conversations were carrying him through the night. Glancing over, I saw him ponder, agree, and disagree with the voices in his head for a while before I decided to interrupt.

"Wanna banana?" It was a poor attempt to spark a dialogue.

"Nah, I've got a pork rind and some other stuff in my pack," he replied, "Mind if I eat?"

Without waiting for an answer, he reached back and started rummaging through his sack.

This is going to be a long haul, I thought. *No radio, no caffeine, and a guy who chews on pork rinds. Hope his story is an interesting one.* The little whorls of snow on the road were starting to stick, and the taillights ahead of me had slowed to a crawl.

Hiddle muttered something incoherent, and then abruptly turned to me and asked, "No radio, huh?"

"Nope. Bought this vehicle for a few bills from a guy who manages a junkyard in New Hampshire. I guess he stripped the extras."

"So what d'you do to stay awake?" He had obviously decided to fill the silence with conversation.

"Oh, I dunno. Roll the windows down. Roll the windows up. Drink a lot of caffeine, do isometrics, think a lot. I'm working on a book right now, so sometimes I try to write."

Hiddle yawned. "Yeah? A book? What's it about?" He tipped his seat back.

I regretted the comment instantly. "It's a collection of stories about climbing in the Himalaya. You know, things that I've done, places I've been, that kind of drizzle," I replied, guarded and glad that he didn't seem interested. "But, hey, don't go to sleep on me. I need someone to talk to so I don't plow over some hitchhiker standing at the side of the road."

"Tell me one of those stories, then." He had his hands folded behind his head and elbows splayed in a position that I found disarmingly at ease. I wasn't used to hitchhikers making themselves so, well, *comfortable* in my car.

"I can't just yank a story out of the abyss," I protested. "You need to ask me an interesting question. You have to tell me what kind of story you want to hear or something."

He thought for a moment. "O.K. How about this...have you ever thought about people who might wear your underwear after you die?"

I stared at him. *I think my mother or somebody once warned me about guys like this,* I thought. But the question and his blasé, presumptuous familiarity amused me. And I figured I probably had enough material for a story on the topic of postmortem underwear acquisition, based on an experience I had on an expedition a few years ago.

Which is how I happened to spend twelve hours telling him about the moths on the glacier, the game of falling things, and the labyrinth.

"THE STORY OF THE DEAD MAN'S UNDERWEAR TAKES PLACE, like any good New Age myth, in a place full of non-English names," I began. "Once upon a time, high on a mountain called

Gasherbrum, deep in the Karakoram range of the Himalaya, a little over half a mile from the Indo-Pakistani border, there were two Spanish climbers, huddled in a tent. There was a storm outside, and they were miserable. They had reached the summit of the mountain already, but they had somehow wandered off-route on the descent. In the flat white light of the storm they hadn't been able to find the top of a chute of ice called the Japanese couloir. One of them had fallen several hundred feet, and he was lying in the tent with a serious back injury, unable to move his feet and legs."

Only the story wasn't a myth. The two climbers were Alfonso Juez and Manuel Alvarez, members of a Spanish military expedition on a mountain called Gasherbrum I, one of the world's highest peaks, in 1996. They were caught at Camp 3, at 23,000 feet, waiting for a break in the storm, struggling to ward off the inevitable effects of subzero temperatures, high winds, and insufficient oxygen, in a layer of the atmosphere that is often dubbed the "death zone."

Sixty-seven men and one woman were aware of their predicament, but at a distance of six thousand vertical feet and seven horizontal miles, we were completely unable to help. The best we could do was to congregate in the expedition's mess tent at the base of the mountain and listen to Alfonso's panicky, breathless reports, blurred by the crackle of the radio. Two rescue teams were dispatched, but they had no luck. Alfonso's reports became plaintive cries.

We were near the end of the game when the colonel suddenly jumped up, knocked the table, and sent several pieces flying.

He rushed to the radio transmitter—a little black box in the corner of the tent that was emitting a stream of panic, punctuated by bursts of static and terse, shouted responses.

A jumbled picture emerged. When the weather cleared, Alfonso had covered his frostbitten fingers and summoned enough energy to begin the long and precarious process of lowering Manuel down the icy slope. A team of rescuers from Camp 2 had climbed up to meet him, but barely 50 yards above the point at which they would have met, Alfonso slipped. He and Manuel careened down the couloir, cartwheeling in a hapless, exhausted tangle of limbs, and landed in a heap only feet from their teammates.

Manuel was dead.

I left quietly and retreated to my own tent wondering how Manuel's wife, at home in Spain with their one-year-old daughter, would receive the news.

Two days later, one of the climbers who had climbed up to bury Manuel's body, Iñaki Ochoa, stopped by my tent, wearing a pair of long blue tights that I knew weren't his. I didn't know it then, but his visit was to become the catalyst for a dream that would return to me two years later, on another expedition, with another climber, and another pair of blue tights.

"You're wearing Manuel's underwear," I said, unable to disguise the curiosity and surprise in my voice. "Where did they come from?"

"From his bag of equipment, of course." Iñaki laughed, shaking his head at my bewilderment. "Do you think we would undress him before we buried him?" Manuel's wife didn't want his equipment shipped back to Spain, he explained. Various members of the expedition were wearing his extra clothing, possibly as a tribute to Manuel, or maybe because it was cleaner than their own.

"Do you want to wear these?" he offered.

"No, thanks. I'm going to do laundry as soon as it stops snowing, and those probably haven't been washed in three weeks," I added hastily.

The disposal of a body or clothing wasn't new to me, but I had never encountered this paying-homage-to-the-dead-by-wearing-underwear custom before. It was an oddly intimate gesture, one that somehow underscored the similarity between Iñaki's living body and Manuel's dead one. It was a whim that made the death seem so real in my mind.

That night the conversation with Iñaki took root and ripened into a vivid dream. In it there was a body, lying in a transparent sleeping bag, skin and clothes and bag all fused together in a decomposing vacuolar goo. A dozen climbers were lowering the body slowly into a crevasse in the snow, smiling and jeering and throwing pristine white underwear down on top of the body. I edged closer and closer, trying to see who it was. The growing bubble of terror inside me erupted in a flood of relief when I glimpsed enough of the body to know that it wasn't me.

The dream faded away, and I woke in a bath of sweat, my skin sticking to the nylon lining of my sleeping bag.

SEVERAL DAYS AFTER THE UNDERWEAR DREAM, I WAS JOLTED out of another dream by the crunch of boots in the snow outside. I was in a different tent this time, at Camp 1, on a plateau of snow at 19,000 feet, near where Manuel's body had been buried.

I crawled halfway out of the back vestibule to have a look at the climbers who had just arrived, before sunrise, in a snowstorm. Two men were standing and pointing in the direction of Base Camp.

"What you do-eeng here?" the taller one exclaimed, his voice squeaking with surprise.

"Climbing," I replied, groggy from lack of sleep and slightly annoyed at the question. They tromped on.

I pulled my shoulders back into the tent and shook the snow off my hat. "What was that all about? I haven't even seen those two before," I grumbled to my tent mate.

He laughed. "Don't take it personally, Heidi. They just didn't know how to react when they saw a woman's head sticking out of the tent. There's probably no other female climber within a 100-mile radius of here."

I hadn't thought of that. I poked my head out again. They had stopped a mere 10 feet beyond our tent.

"Well, there's no other tent within a 100 foot radius of here, and they've decided to pitch their tent right on our back door step," I announced.

Curiosity had wiped the urge to sleep from my body. I pulled my mitts on and began melting a pot of snow to make a meal to bring over.

TWO POTS OF WATER LATER I WAS SITTING IN THE TENT with the newcomers, two Ukrainian climbers. The taller one introduced himself as Vladislav "Slavas" Terzyoul. I recognized the name from the annals of Himalayan climbing, a genuine Ukrainian "hard man." Only two years prior, Slavas had been a member of a small but strong team of Ukrainian climbers on K2, arguably the hardest of the 8,000-meter peaks. It had been a good season. A Basque team had succeeded in establishing a new route on the south-southeast spur in June, and Everest guide Rob Hall had managed to reach the summit with supplemental oxygen in early July. And then, on July 11, three of Slavas's teammates, Dmitri, Alexsei, and Aleksandr, had disappeared on their descent.

After two weeks he found two of them, frozen figures hanging off an ice screw, a few hundred feet below the summit in a region of the climb called the Bottleneck. He cut the cord that bound his partners' bodies to their anchor, watched them fall, and then continued on to the summit with his remaining partner, Benko.

"These toes gone on Broad Peak," said the other Ukrainian hard man, Slavas' current partner, pointing at one bare foot. He was sitting with nothing other than a pair of dingy wool briefs on, clearly pleased at having a "lady climber" bring him a breakfast of boil-bag hot dogs and beans.

Slavas was sucking drafts of water from a canteen, waiting for his turn to sample the hot dogs and beans, and staring at me. "You are a leetle Wanda," he said, shaking his head, referring to another female Himalayan climber he had presumably met on a previous expedition.

As we conversed in broken English, an outline of their ambitious plan emerged. They had just arrived at the base of the mountain after a grueling sprint up the glacier, and their intent was to go directly to the summit of an 8,000-meter peak called Gasherbrum II in two days, without acclimatization, ropes, stoves, or any of the usual accoutrements.

"What will you eat with no stove?" I asked, hoping to discover the secret source of energy that fuels this particular brand of climber. Slavas grinned, revealing a gleaming gold incisor, and produced a hunk of some white gelatinous substance.

"Veree good!" he announced, "I made. You eat." He spread a thick slice of it on a hard crust of bread and then added yellow paste from a very small tube labeled "vitaminerales."

I took a bite. The yellow vitaminerale paste was mustard. And the white gelatinous stuff—well, all I could be sure of was that it was some kind of fat.

"Yum. Very good…What animal?" I asked, pointing at the fat.

With the language barrier, the only way to answer the question was through pantomime.

It was a horse.

Pure homemade horse fat, with mustard. On a crust of bread.

Although there are as many theories about what to eat at high altitude as there are climbers and countries, one commonly accepted fact is that a climber's *carte du jour* should blatantly violate the International Heart Association guidelines for healthy living. Pierre Beghin, a famous French climber, climbed with a pocket full of pure salt. Alison Hargreaves, Britain's controversial climber-mother, was known for her ability to pack away freeze-dried cheesecakes and other sweets. Slavas' solution was horse fat.

As we slathered another slice of fat on the bread crust, the radio crackled to life. The Ukrainians' "coach," a rotund guy in a bright pink track suit we had met at Base Camp the day before, came on, directing them to "go for dee summeet *now.*" The slew of military-style commands finally subsided, and Slavas cleared his throat.

"Can you tell me," he asked sheepishly, "weech mountain Jee Too?"

I hesitated, valiantly resisted the urge to direct them to another, harder peak, and pointed instead in the correct direction. It was still snowing out, and GII was veiled by clouds, so my gesture was a vague one, through the wall of the tent.

"Good!" Slavas smiled, unsheathing his knife. "I make a weendow!"

His partner, still sitting in his underwear, instantly produced a quick-draw roll of first-aid tape from the outside pocket of his pack. "You make a weendow, I feex it," he growled, obviously accustomed to Slavas's reckless humor.

I looked from one to the other, barely knowing whether the vagaries of these two climbers from another continent were comedy or a bad dream. It was all so deliciously pointless and inane. Two climbers, obeying the orders of a bellicose pink-suited coach, risking their lives in some remote corner of the world for no particularly good reason. We were fellow travelers, comrades on a march to nowhere.

As I laughed, something in my psyche fused and I understood the wearing-a-dead-man's-underwear thing. Death in the mountains, like life, is a public affair. There is no way of making it remote or clinical or clean. There is no way of neatly packaging a body, sealing it in the past and wrapping the memories up with a pristine obituary for posterity. When a climber dies, his partners continue to climb, recreating his life and sometimes his spirit with each step. The faceless climber that was lowered into the crevasse in my dream had taken everyone's underwear with him.

I turned to Slavas's partner. "Hey," I asked, pointing at his briefs, "Do you have another pair of those?"

I had not set off with the object of conquering a peak nor indeed of returning home a hero. What I wanted was to come to know and understand the fears of the world, and my own fears. I wanted to feel new again.

—REINHOLD MESSNER

FALLING THINGS

The story finished, my mind trailed off into a string of thoughts about the climb that followed that encounter— about sleeping on top of the debris from other expeditions at 25,000 feet, about the hallucinations at Camp 4, about the serrated fin of snow leading to the summit.

Hiddle seemed to be waiting for something. "Yeah?" he asked finally. "So?"

"So what?"

"So did he give you his underwear?"

I groaned. "No, of course not. What a question. I'm sure he didn't understand what I said, anyhow, and I didn't think of pantomiming the request."

"Who were you just thinking of, then?"

"Not *who*. What."

"All right, what were you just thinking about?"

I paused. I had been thinking about a who, I realized, with a sudden lurch of disappointment in my stomach. The who was inextricably tangled with the what.

"I was thinking about our summit bid on that expedition," I explained absently, still mulling through the memories. "You spend weeks, even months, prepping the route, fixing ropes and establishing camps on the lower sections of the mountain, and then the final push boils down to 48 hours of luck. Maybe serendipity is a better word. It's not like you can make the summit through sheer brute will. You have to be in synch with the rhythms of the weather, your body, the mountain."

I stopped. Telling the hitchhiker a about a dead man's underwear and a meal of horse fat was one thing; divulging the messier emotions and experiences of the entire Gasherbrum expedition was another.

I had left for Pakistan in May 1996, after three months of furtively raising money and hiding my climbing equipment from my husband, Zee. A climber himself, Zee had originally supported the idea of the expedition, but had later tried to prevent me from going. He had blocked phone calls from the expedition leader; threatened to shred my down suit with a knife, locked me out of the house when I left to go for a run. Normally when our disagreements led to a barrage of verbal and physical abuse, I simply acquiesced, but in this case I hadn't. The dream of climbing an 8,000-meter peak was too central to my spirit to quit, even if it meant the dissolution of our marriage.

"Go on," Hiddle said, interrupting my thoughts. "I'm listening."

"Hold on, I'm not sure where to begin," I responded, still not sure how much I wanted to share with a stranger.

There *was* a beginning—I think—in the moment I decided, in a hotel in a place called Skardu, to take off my wedding ring. But every time I revisit that scene, trying to remember my thoughts, recalling the conversation with the expedition leader about leaving behind items that I wouldn't want returned to my family if something happened to me, I can find nothing but simple action-and-reaction. Did I decide to leave my ring in Skardu simply in case I didn't return? I didn't know. Driving through the dark and snow, it didn't seem to matter anyhow.

So instead I began the story for the hitchhiker with our departure for the summit of a mountain called Gasherbrum II, or simply GII, one of the 14 highest points on Earth.

"There were four of us left for the summit at about four o'clock one morning in July 1996, after six weeks of fixing ropes and acclimatizing," I explained. "You can't go straight to the summit. At 27,000 feet, the pressure is less than a third of the normal pressure at sea level. There's so little oxygen at that altitude that without undergoing the physiological changes that occur during the acclimitization process, you'd die in about five minutes. So you spend weeks going up and down the route, pushing incrementally higher, a few thousand feet each time, and then returning to Base Camp to allow your body to recoup and generate new red blood cells. It can be an exhausting process. And of course there's the constant threat of avalanches and storms every time you go up, so it's easy to get worn down by the risk factors. By the end of July, most of the members of my team had dropped out, and I was climbing with a loose-knit group of individuals—a French climber named Jean-Christophe LaFaille, a Basque climber named José Carlos

Tamayo, and a Spanish guy named Ramon Portilla."

After weeks of carrying packs laden with ropes, tents, fuel, and food, we felt weightless, exuberant as we left Base Camp for what we hoped would be the final push to the summit. I remember running through the ice fall, crossing crevasses, the deep cracks that span bulges in the glacier like furrows in a forehead, unroped, without the usual fears or hesitation. I remember watching Jean-Chri, running ahead of me, as he flew across a chasm, plunged his axe into the vertical ice on the other side, scrambled up the wall of the crevasse, and continued running. I remember feeling sanguine, invulnerable. We covered seven miles and 3,000 vertical feet in a breathless 54 minutes.

As we reached Camp 1, Tamayo and Ramon, saddled with film equipment for the Spanish television station TVE, decided to rest for a few minutes and melt snow for water. I opted to stay with them, and Jean-Chri decided to try to "flash" the route, to climb the 40 or so remaining hours to the summit of Gasherbrum II without stopping in an established camp.

Ten hours later, Tamayo, Ramon, and I radioed back to Iñaki, who had stayed behind at Base Camp. "We're at Camp 2," we informed him.

Iñaki had already reached the summit of nearby GI in early July.

"I'm coming up to join you," he responded.

We all grinned. After a day of restless pacing at Base Camp, Iñaki had obviously succumbed to the temptation of climbing with us.

"You go on ahead," I suggested to Tamayo and Ramon, "I'll wait for Iñaki and brew up some extra water. We'll catch up with you at Camp 4."

Ten hours later, Iñaki and I were struggling up over the final lip of ice to Camp 4. Every step was deliberate, a conscious effort to make neurons in our addled brains fire, to turn intent and desire into action. There was a thin rope, I noticed in a detached, dim way, a shoe string, leading up through the rime-covered rocks. The sheath was bleached bone-white by UV rays and frayed through to the core in places. Farther up was a pair of boots, toes pointed up, attached to a snow-covered red suit. The body of a climber, probably the Austrian who had died in 1982.

On the slope above, I could see Tamayo carefully picking through the debris with an ice axe, looking for a sleeping mat. Beyond Tamayo, up in the clouds, was a little moving speck in the snow: Jean-Chri descending from the summit. Perfect weather, perfect snow conditions. My heart soared.

"HOW DID THE AUSTRIAN DIE?" HIDDLE WANTED TO KNOW.

"I'm not sure. Exposure to altitude, I guess. There are some nasty side effects of spending time at altitudes above 23,000 feet—strokes, heart attacks, retinal hemorrhages, that sort of thing. He was at 25,000 feet. There's not enough air at that level for a helicopter to hover, which makes rescue or retrieval of a body impossible. Camp 4 on this particular mountain isn't scoured by high winds or avalanches, the way many of the other high camps are, so it's a sort of high-altitude graveyard."

WE SPENT ABOUT NINE HOURS MELTING SNOW, AN HOUR and a half for each liter, and then settled into a restless five-hour nap. I woke an hour before midnight, in a dreamless, queasy state of lethargy. Iñaki was awake too. "I'm losing my left foot," he mumbled. "Can you try to warm it on your stomach?" We numbly contorted ourselves into a pretzel of down suits and plastic boots, held the position until other limbs started to lose circulation, and then shifted again.

Our bodies were rapidly disintegrating, and the awareness that each hour at altitude means millions of dead cells pierced the fog in my brain in random intervals of mild panic. "This is crazy. We should brew up and go now," I heard myself say.

After another hour of fitful dozing, an hour of melting chipped ice for one water bottle, and an hour of melting more chipped ice for the other bottle, we went out into the night, slowly, methodically following the dim circles of our headlamps up through the crystalline snow and brain-numbing cold.

Sometime in the middle of the night, I paused, listening to a nagging voice within me, and turned around. Behind us, 100 miles away, sheets of lightning were radiating out from a peak. I stopped and stared at it, wondering if I was hallucinating.

Hallucinations are common on high peaks. Frank Smythe, one of the early Everest climbers, tried to feed half of his mint cake to an imaginary partner at around 23,000 feet. Peter Habeler, one of the first two climbers to reach the summit of Everest without supplemental oxygen, was troubled for days after the ascent by apparitions of insects and worms filling his tent at Base Camp, around 16,700 feet. And Doug Scott and Dougal Haston, the first climbers to succeed on the southwest face of Everest, found themselves having conversations with illusory companions in a snow cave at nearly 29,000 feet.

Maybe the hallucinations are caused by oxygen deprivation. Maybe your brain gets a little tweaked when you climb without sleeping for a couple of days. Or maybe something more happens, something deeper. It's hard to talk about "hearing voices on the mountain" without sounding like a gibbering fool, so most of the time it's easier to avoid the topic. Climbers who do attempt to describe the experience usually describe either a state of mental detachment, or a state of deep clarity and connectedness.

As I held my breath and squinted into the darkness, I saw another flash of light and knew, with a sudden quiet awe, that it was real. There were no clouds in any quarter of our three-dimensional horizon, so it couldn't have been a storm. The lightning must be a bizarre electrical disturbance in the atmosphere, I reasoned, visible only from above. I leaned into the slope and twisted around farther to survey the rest of the panorama. It was something beyond my textbook comprehension of the physical world, some phenomenon that transcended my meager understanding of the universe. I have seen this type of high-altitude aurora borealis on two other 8,000-meter peaks since then. On Kanchenjunga it looked like the arcs of static electricity you see in those glass plasma balls, snaking and floating through atmosphere in pink and purple-blue cracks, scissures in the ionosphere.

Realizing that there is a distance between what you know you have seen and what you know is possible inspires a humble, reverent sort of feeling. And so as the sea of blue peaks below emerged from the darkness and the atmosphere grew thinner, I prayed to the rocks.

Prayer seemed like the natural, maybe even the necessary, mode for conversing with all the spirits in the air.

Praying to a rock seemed easier than praying directly to God, because there was nearly always a rock nearby.

"THERE'S A CONCEPT IN ANCIENT INDIAN MYTHOLOGY called Ananku," the hitchhiker remarked. "I think it's a Tamil belief, a belief in a sacred power that exists in dangerous places such as chasms and waterfalls, and dangerous animals like snakes and tigers. A power that lures victims into the danger."

I waited for him to say more, but he seemed intent on digging something out of his backpack again. More pork rinds probably. Was he trying to suggest that there was danger, "Ananku," on the slopes of the mountain, or in the bizarre electrical disturbances in the atmosphere? I wasn't sure.

Just then the car started to skid on a long patch of black ice. I instinctively hit the brakes, precisely the wrong thing to do. We rocketed over the section sideways, heading for a ditch, and then reached terra firma a fraction of a second before either of us realized how nearly fatal that experience had been.

"Yeah, well, that stretch of road was loaded with Ananku," I commented. Hiddle let out a nervous chuckle and ran his fingers through his hair.

THE SPIRITUAL, OTHERWORLDLY FEELING PERSISTED AS WE continued upward, and in the hour before the sun rose on the upper flanks of the mountain, in that blue hour before dawn, I paused again to turn around and survey the clouds below peeling back to reveal jagged ridges and flutes of ice. Somehow each chiseled, vibrant detail of the landscape below seemed both remote and intimate, as though spatial distances no longer had any real meaning, as though I could, if I wanted to, reach out and caress the sharpness of that peak over there, or the warmth of that lone star drifting in the wash of the blue near the horizon. As I leaned on the shaft of my ice axe, gasping in the cold air, both my mind and my body felt strangely unencumbered, boundless. That pillar of rock jutting up from the slope? My thumb. The crevasses in the glacier below? Folds in my skin. I felt certain that I could fly anywhere if I wanted to, but there was no need to fly because the unsteady pulse of the entire Earth was the same as my own.

I turned and started kicking my boots into the snow again.

After many thousands of identical steps we finally reached the top of the slope and threw our arms over a beautifully thin fin of snow, a six-inch-wide tightrope swooping more than 300 feet through empty space to the summit. The snow to the left of the ridge was bathed in the amber glow of the sunrise; on the right, it was still purple from the night. I hefted one leg over the side in shadow and studied the dropoff on both sides carefully. I'd fall about 3,000 feet on the Pakistani side, 2,000 feet on the Chinese side. Best to lean slightly toward the Chinese side, the rational side of my brain decided on some dim, detached level.

And as I sat there straddling the ridge, I started to laugh. Some of the international borders on Earth are ridges. Perched on a drift of snow that thaws and melts and shifts with the seasons, the concept of international boundaries seemed ridiculous. The only boundaries that seemed to matter were the vertical ones, the ones that separate layers of air with enough oxygen from those without, life from death.

My fragmented thoughts were interrupted by a sudden noise. Over there: falling rock. For a few long moments the black shape somersaulted down the purple side of the ridge, bounding and rebounding in slow motion, before it ricocheted off the cliff at the bottom and disappeared. I shook my head, as if it might shake the vision of falling things from my brain, and shrugged. Struggling for each lungful of oxygen in these regions of the troposphere, you somehow assume the rules of gravity do not apply to you, as long as you are still alive. The real problem isn't how to avoid falling. It's how to avoid becoming a falling thing.

"Ananku," Hiddle said suddenly.

"What?"

"That's what I was trying to tell you about before. That power, Ananku. It's Ananku that lures you into the void, pulls you down, transforms you into a falling thing. You ever felt like something was trying to pull you over the edge?"

"Maybe, I don't know. I can't remember feeling like anything was pulling me down, but I'm not even sure I can remember crossing that ridge," I confessed. "I guess intense concentration can somehow block the receptors for memory. I remember standing on the summit, of course, feeling strong, but tentative, reminding myself that we were only halfway. The trick isn't getting to the top, it's getting back down. I remember spending an entire hour or so up there, just staring at a route called the Abruzzi Ridge on another peak, a mountain called K2 that is about 10 miles as the crow flies from GII. Somehow the ridge looked really do-able, even easy, which just proves that my brain was suffering from the effects of oxygen deprivation."

I stopped talking, and Hiddle didn't respond, so I let my mind drift back down the more complex paths of the emotions during and after the climb. My relationship with Iñaki, I am sure, was what gave me the strength to put the ring back on in Skardu, to return to Zee after the expedition. It gave me parity. It gave Zee the satisfaction of a righteous, justified anger.

I THOUGHT ABOUT THE FIRST NIGHT IÑAKI AND I SHARED A tent. It was the night after Manuel died.

He had caught my wrist gently as I left the mess tent after the radio call. "Are you all right? " he had asked. The probing look in his eyes filled me with desire.

We wrapped ourselves into an inseparable knot that night, collapsing inside each other. I thought about Manuel and the evanescence of life.

"*Mi media naranja*," Iñaki whispered to me at three o'clock in the morning. He had just pulled on his boots and was about to leave with the other members of his team who were going up to bury Manuel's body.

"Your media naranja? Your half orange?" I mumbled sleepily, not understanding.

"The other half of my fruit, the other half of my soul," he whispered and kissed me on the forehead.

"Mmm," I closed my eyes and smiled.

It was a relationship that was loaded with—what did the hitchhiker call it? Ananku?—a relationship that was dangerous, a relationship that lured us over the edge into the realm of falling things.

If love is the answer, could you rephrase the question?

—LILY TOMLIN

IÑAKI

When I returned home to Zee in September 1996, I told him that I had fallen in love with Iñaki. It wasn't an easy thing to do. Our daughter Devi was three. She had spent the summer with my parents while I climbed and Zee completed a forestry internship in Washington state.

I was worried about how my decision to leave Zee would affect her.

I was even more worried about what would happen if we stayed together.

We had been married for five years. For four of those five years, I had been struggling to keep an escalating spiral of abuse and deception and anger in check.

Things weren't always so crazy, of course. In the beginning, our relationship was founded on trust.

As climbing partners, we had learned to entrust our lives to each other and the rope that connected us. We goaded each other to the limits, cultivated private jokes, and crossed the border of fear without ever quite reaching the boundary of terror. We honed our skills on the walls of Yosemite, where Zee worked on the SAR climbing team; in the Rockies; on the ice of New England; and on the glaciers and peaks of the Alps. Climbing was more than a sport; it was a shared lifestyle, a religion. We practiced the art of minimalism, scrounging scrap metal and seatbelts from the junkyard to make the hanging platform we needed for our escapes into vast vertical oceans of ice and granite.

We hugged each other on the summit of the Matterhorn during our honeymoon. The world was ours. And then, barely four months after we were married, I was pregnant.

I was twenty-three. It didn't seem young at the time. Everything in my life up to then had happened in an accelerated fashion. I had graduated from high school at age seventeen, studied mathematics and philosophy at Wellesley College for three years, and then been invited to start the graduate program in philosophical logic at M.I.T. At age twenty-one, I had been accepted into the program with a five-year fellowship for the Ph.D. track.

After the first year, I decided to take a year off to wait for a mathematics professor I wanted to work with to return from a sabbatical in Jerusalem.

In that year, I lived alone in a cabin on a lake in New Hampshire, traveled and climbed, raced in triathlons, coached swimming, read the entire works of Thoreau and Emerson, got married, and got pregnant.

The concept of raising a child while working full time and completing my Ph.D. seemed very manageable.

What I didn't count on was the energy it would take to keep Zee's resentment in check.

I DON'T THINK I REALIZED HOW VOLATILE OUR MARRIAGE was until one hot and thundery morning in July 1993. Devi was ten months old, and I had found a reasonable job as an aquatics director at an outdoor recreation complex in the Boston area. Normally I brought her to work with me, and either carried her around in a backpack or let her toddle around with the older kids on my swim team. This particular morning, though, Zee had the day off.

As I pulled my work clothes on, the clouds outside collided in a flash of light and long rumbling growl.

Devi was awake, watching me get ready.

"Ooma," she said, banging her hands on the bed and then reaching them out to me, "I uv oo."

It was the first time she had said I love you. I felt a knot of emotion in my throat, and decided to take her with me.

"You do not," Zee said through clenched teeth, "need to go to work today."

"Don't worry, I'll take Dev," I responded quickly.

"No." He picked her up and pocketed the set of car keys lying on the dresser.

I started to explain that I *did* have a responsibility to go in, even though it was raining, at least for an hour or two to unlock the door for a corporate meeting and ask one or two of the staff members to stay. Then I saw the fury in his eyes, and stopped. By then I knew better than to contradict him or aggravate him when he was in one of these moods.

Best to do what I needed to do and come home as quickly as possible, I reasoned.

I pretended to go down to the kitchen to put some water on to boil. When I was sure he hadn't followed me, I grabbed a spare set of car keys by the door and ran out into the rain.

I hadn't been quick or quiet enough.

Zee caught up with me outside in the driveway, threw the car door open, grabbed my shirt and hair, and dragged me back up the steps into the kitchen.

I started to scream, and he instinctively put his hands around my neck, closing them tighter and tighter, until the screaming stopped.

I was sobbing when I regained consciousness. I couldn't talk. Both my larynx and my emotions were bruised. I was silent for the next week, and the week after that.

I didn't have the courage to leave; I didn't have the courage to stay.

Three weeks later, I invited a friend from college to lunch. She was dating a computer engineer from Harvard who wore bow ties to her a cappella performances. He played the saxophone and liked to listen to David Brubeck while they were in bed.

"Heidi," she said, "you can't imagine what it's like with some-one who has the lips of a saxophonist."

I nodded and decided not to try to imagine it.

This is what I told her about Zee: We had qualified for free milk and cheese on his income, so I had gone back to work full-time; he cooked loving, delicious dinners full of meat, which I ate because it didn't seem worth the trouble to remind him that I was vegetarian; he had almost killed me, but it was an accident (he just didn't realize his own strength, I told her), and I didn't have the courage to leave him. I said this all between small bites of asparagus au gratin and games of pat-a-cake with Devi.

My friend asked me why I felt I couldn't leave. Maybe there was something I could do to prevent the outbursts, I argued. What I really meant was that divorce was failure and I had never had to admit defeat before.

During that luncheon, I toyed with different rationalizations until I persuaded myself that the real problem was that Zee and I had such different backgrounds. Zee had been raised in a two-bedroom house with five siblings; I had been raised in a five-bedroom house with one sibling. He wasn't sure whether he had graduated from high school; I had been working on a Ph.D.

The solution seemed obvious, and simple. I needed to help him get an undergraduate degree.

I coaxed him into auditing a university-level geology class with me, and helped him write application essays. I taught him to spell words like college, and student. In July of 1994, we moved to Corvallis, Oregon. I found a job as a technical writer, and Zee began a four-year program in forestry management at Oregon State University.

We juggled work and studying, parenting and climbing. He seemed happy, most of the time. But the violence and sporadic explosions of anger didn't stop. Over a period of two years, we lost two sets of housemates, couples who were upset by the way he treated both them and me.

By the time I left to climb Gasherbrum, I think I was looking for a new life.

Iñaki, with all his gentleness and apparent compassion, seemed to provide it.

BUT LEAVING WHEN YOU HAVE A CHILD, I DISCOVERED, IS not as simple as walking out. After I told him about Iñaki, Zee threatened to disappear with Devi, to take her to the Armenian village where he was born, in Syria. You'll never see her again, he warned.

Weary from the expedition and worried about financial issues, I simply agreed to stay.

WE DESTROYED EVERYTHING. ZEE WENT THROUGH ALL OF MY slides from the expedition, one by one, and held a lighter underneath each one he thought might be a reminder of Iñaki. He found the slip of paper with the phone number printed in Iñaki's meticulous left-handed slant and flushed it down the toilet. He noticed the way I put my hand over the black-and-white *xi* stone on the leather cord around my neck. He tore it off and sent it flying into a pile of dry brown leaves.

I watched and didn't try to stop him. Guilt was a new emotion for me then, and his violence purged it in a strangely satisfying way.

All of the evidence was erased, but history wasn't. Flipping through an old issue of *Climbing Magazine* a month after I came home from the GII expedition, I stumbled on a photograph of a climber, anonymous, lying on a stretcher at Base Camp on the north side of K2, his left arm bandaged in a huge plaster cast.

It was Iñaki. His face was ugly after the fall.

On K2, two years prior, he had pulled on an old fixed line that snapped and sent him flying, falling through space. He hadn't known that the rope would break. Did he realize that the events of the expedition on GII would lead inevitably to another fall? He had just gotten married, two months before the expedition, to a beautiful climber in Spain. They had gone trekking in Nepal, in the Annapurna sanctuary, for their honeymoon, and then he had come directly to Pakistan, to GII. I felt his hands on my shoulders, his eyes looking at me sadly, desperately, his lips saying I love you for the hundredth time. He must have known.

I put the magazine in the bathroom, flipped it open and let my emotions hang naked when I knew the door was locked. That cast on his arm—that cast had become soggy on his journey back home to Spain, riding camels across the braided rivers in the Shaksgam Valley, on the north side of K2. The cast went all the way from his shoulder to the knuckles of his left hand. Was that hand, his writing hand, immobilized after this fall, too? I hoped it was. Some things are better left unsaid. And the black-and-white xi stone that must have been around his neck, hidden beneath the folds of that blanket—that was the same stone Zee had thrown into the leaves. I touched the hollow above my clavicle, and felt the weight of the stone in a lump in my throat. Did he feel the same heavy emptiness around his neck? Those eyebrows furrowed in pain in the photograph—didn't he break a rib in the fall on K2? The fingers in my memory traced a small, smooth lump on his back. It must have rebroken, and pierced his heart.

Finally I cut the photo out. I sent the original to Iñaki, and tucked a gray-and-white photocopy, a ghost of the original, into a little white envelope. I sealed the envelope hesitantly, wondering if I'd be able to resist the impulse to open it again.

Then I buried it in a gray drawer in the gray desk in the gray cubicle where I worked, at a company called Summit Information Systems.

I THOUGHT I WAS DOING THE RIGHT THING AT THE TIME. I had no way of knowing that the violence would escalate beyond me. No way of knowing that it would lead to rocks falling from the sky, an axe cutting a rope, a near tragedy on K2.

Until one is committed there is hesitancy, the chance to draw back, always ineffectiveness. Concerning all acts of initiative (and creation), there is one elementary truth, the ignorance of which kills countless ideas and splendid plans: that the moment one definitely commits oneself, then Providence moves too. All sorts of things occur to help one that would never otherwise have occurred.

— W. H. Murray

GESTATION

The actual origins of the ambition to climb K2 are unclear. Maybe the dream was conceived during that hour I stood on the summit of Gasherbrum, gazing at the flanks of K2. Or maybe it began in childhood, as I watched a female climber in a documentary about the search for Noah's Ark and realized that girls could climb, too. Or perhaps the trip was an attempt to find closure in a failing marriage, to either heal the wounds or finalize the separation. I'll never know. What is clear is that some time in the summer of 1997, I decided to apply for a permit to climb K2.

Other mountains share with K2 a history of adventure, triumph, and tragedy, but only K2 can claim the title of the Savage Mountain, the mountaineer's mountain, the most formidable hunk of ice and rock in the world. As the second highest and one of the most remote peaks on Earth, it has either claimed the lives or exacted a high price from all of the women and many of the men who have tried to reach its 28,250-foot (8,611-meter) summit. Five women have reached the top, but only three of those returned. Both of the two who succeeded, a Polish climber named Wanda Rutkiewicz and a French climber named Chantal Manduit, survived frostbite and brutal conditions on the descent. "I knew K2 would somehow mark the rest of my life," Wanda commented years after her ascent. "My reaction to aggression, disaster, or tragedy is delayed. There are events that I have lived but still can't fully accept." The primitive, often desperate struggles that unfold in the high realms of the Himalaya are reason enough to view any of its giant peaks as an adventure into the unknown, an irresistible challenge. But the unique history of K2 has elevated it to something more—to a symbol of courage and endurance, an incomparable test of the body and spirit. It is the ultimate goal for many climbers, and reaching the summit is akin to winning the Olympic gold.

K2, K2, K2! The word has been part of my now-eight-year-old daughter's vocabulary since she was three. So I suppose it was no surprise that the conversation with the hitchhiker led inexorably to the topic of my attempt to climb the mountain in 1998.

"GROWTH IS A FUNNY THING. HAVE YOU EVER WATCHED the leaves on trees in the spring, or a flower unfolding? Or the fingernails of a child?" I asked Hiddle, as though he had been following the twisted path of my thoughts. "Natural growth isn't linear, you know. There's an irregular rhythm to it, like the patterns in the surf, or the throb of an artery. Each spurt is followed by a lull, a pause, before the next surge." He gave me an odd look, and I realized that I was talking to him like an old friend. I needed to back off, ask him a question about his own life, as any socially functional person would.

I switched course abruptly. "Do you have kids?"

"No." He tipped his seat back and stared out the passenger window, clearly surprised by my blunt question.

I probably should've shut up, but somehow I felt a need to patch the awkward silence.

"You know what I mean with the way things grow in surges?" He nodded. "It was a random comment, I know. I was thinking about an expedition that I organized two years after the Gasherbrum trip, an expedition to K2. I'm not even sure I can really remember how the concept of climbing K2 got started. I just remember how the whole crazy idea grew until it had a life of its own, like having a kid."

The months preceding a Himalayan expedition are a gestation period. For a while the expedition is just a dream, germinating in the fertile soil of desire, nurtured maybe by an enthusiastic co-dreamer and a dozen or so odd books and maps. Then the first burst of growth happens. The team comes together, the permit arrives, the T-shirts or other paraphernalia are printed, your efforts to find sponsors suddenly bear the first fruit. Almost overnight the dream magically morphs into a real-life miracle.

Some time between conception and the actual birth, during the long laborious months of mental visualization, reflection, and physical training, there is the point at which you realize how naive your original dream was. Then comes the moment when you realize that you yourself are really just a peripheral detail, that the expedition has acquired a heartbeat of its own.

And then there's the growth at the end of the gestation period, the time when the sheer weight of beast—especially the expedition logistics—begins to feel burdensome. The whole process loses its aura of miracle and mystery. The cascade of boxes on your doorstep, the astounding leaps and bounds in your phone bill, the anxious and repetitive questioning from family members and media—somehow none of these phenomena strike you as a miracle. You begin to feel invaded by the creature you have created.

"There was the whole media thing, for example," I told Hiddle. "I never wanted K2 to be a news event, but somehow in the process of looking for sponsors, the media factor developed a life of its own. It got to the point where, in the week or two before we left, I was so impatient and restless that I couldn't sleep, so sick of talking about climbing and ready to actually climb that I could barely function."

I smiled as I described one of the last interviews I had done. Jeff Blumenfeld, the PR agent for a website I had agreed to write for, called to inform me that I had a date the following morning in New York City with *The Today Show*. "But, Jeff," I had objected, "I barely know what *The Today Show* is. I don't own a TV. I'm culturally and socially illiterate, remember? I don't even have a car right now—I cancelled my car insurance last week so I can afford life insurance for the expedition."

I could picture him rolling his eyes. "Glad to hear you'll do it," he replied, "I'll drive, and I'll explain what *The Today Show* is on the way there. Be ready at 3:00 a.m., and bring some of your equipment."

The footage from that news clip shows me smiling in bemused disbelief as I watched a very svelte interviewer in Gucci shoes squeeze into my tiny 2.5-pound summit tent. The little zip in the back is for emptying a pee bottle, I explained, trying to sound dainty. To cook, you hang a stove from the top pole, and push the walls of the tent away from it so that the whole thing doesn't disintegrate in one big hot puff. The L and R marks on my boots? Those are so that I can figure out which foot they go on when my brain succumbs to mind fog at 25,000 feet. On the caffeine-fueled ride home, I put my feet up on Jeff's dashboard and welcomed the upcoming 30-hour flight to Pakistan. Anything to escape civilization.

"Why K2 instead of Everest?" Hiddle interrupted.

The question caught me off guard. Among mountaineers, the fact that K2 falls short of Everest as the highest point on Earth by a mere 785 feet is often considered a mere oversight, proof of divine injustice. The summit has been triangulated and re-triangulated, measured and re-measured by teams of mountaineers and geologists using modern surveying techniques with lasers and satellite transmissions, all secretly hoping that there has been some sort of an error. K2, with its sheer black faces and gracefully fluted slopes of snow, is both more beautiful and much more difficult than its rival. Everest quite simply doesn't deserve to be higher.

"Because there are fewer climbers on it, and because you actually fix your own ropes on K2," I replied testily. "Everest has been profaned by the swarms of guided clients. Sherpas typically do almost all the work of setting and maintaining ropes for climbers, at least on the south side. On the south side of K2 there were only 11 of us in the final summit bid, and every one of us had contributed to the leading and fixing ropes."

At the tone of my voice, Hiddle glanced over at me with the hint of a smile and one eyebrow raised. I changed the subject.

"Choosing the team for a Himalayan expedition is hard. You never really know how people will respond to altitude. I had been promising my husband, Zee, that we would go on an 8,000-meter expedition together for two years, so I knew I had to include him. The thing that made choosing the team tricky was that we were already separated—I was living on the East Coast with our daughter, Devi, while he finished his degree in Oregon—and I knew the interpersonal dynamics on the expedition would probably be, well, less than optimal. I wanted one, possibly two, other climbers, but it had to be the right person. It had to be someone who knew Zee and me, somebody who could laugh at Zee's tirades and wouldn't be partial to either of us. So we ended up inviting this guy that Zee knew, a Swiss climber named Chris Binggeli."

"This sounds like the beginnings of a good story," Hiddle said approvingly.

"I guess it is," I grinned, "But it would take a while to tell the whole thing."

"I've got time."

I DECIDED TO BEGIN THE STORY OF THE "K2 98" EXPEDITION for Hiddle in Rawalpindi, that sprawling metropolis of army barracks, rug vendors, and furniture carvers in the heart of Pakistan's lowlands. Home to approximately six million people, Pindi is the usual departure point for expeditions heading to the Karakoram Range. It is also a welcome haven of civilization for weary climbers on the return journey.

Ah, Pindi! Its inhabitants move with the casual air of the prescient. Today they have baked, talked, swept, and bargained; tomorrow they will do the same. Every now and then there are riots, political debacles, and military coups, but even these occur with a certain predictable regularity.

Midnight on June 22, 1998, I decided, was the point to begin the tale. The U.S. missile attack was still two months away, the military coup had yet to be conceived by General Musharraf, and the city was comfortably asleep. I was squatting on the tarpaper roof of the Shalimar Hotel. The chaotic noises of the city, bicycle bells and horses and taxi horns and jitneys, had subsided, and a bat was flying around trying to catch bugs illuminated in the beam of my headlamp.

We'd had a busy day, Zee, Chris, and I, sorting, packing, repacking barrels of climbing equipment into 25-kilogram loads. My head was buzzing with the details of canned tuna, kerosene, and soap, calculations of rupees, dollars, and quantities—everything we would need to survive for three months on a glacier, everything we would need to climb K2. Swirling among these thoughts was that miasma of an Asian city: fresh cloves and cumin, a block of ice on a bicycle rack melting in the midday heat, a cemetery overgrown with wild cannabis, mass halitosis, ripe fruit. It is a world that is moving all the time and yet never changing.

Somewhere in the midst of packing the solar power system and the ropes that morning, I had remembered a small paper bag full of pitons—sitting in the corner of a storage shed in Oregon. They should have been in the barrel with the ice screws, and they weren't. I knew immediately they had been forgotten. Pitons, those pieces of metal climbers hammer in rock faces to anchor ropes, are absolutely essential to the climb. There are all kinds of pitons, with names that describe the shapes—knife blades, bongs, Z-pins— but none of them can be purchased in the open-air markets or corner stores of Rawalpindi. The Pakistani climber helping us with arrangements for our trip, Ashraf Aman, had been able to loan us a couple of bongs and assorted pins, but I knew they weren't going to be enough.

So I found myself at midnight, sitting cross-legged with a furrowed brow on the roof of the hotel, trying to forget the pitons and focusing instead on a black box in my lap. It was a thing of the future, a machine that could communicate with telephones on the other side of the world. A "mini-M satellite phone," the tech gurus back in the U.S. had called it. I was using it to fill a voicemail box half a world away with an update that would be posted on the Internet. Although I was dressed in traditional Pakistani garb for women, a loose *shalwar kameez* and *dopatta* that covered my arms, hair, and any other indecent parts, I couldn't help looking about nervously. Common sense told me that women in Pakistan don't usually pick locks on doors and climb up on roofs at midnight to make phone calls with black boxes.

My fears were well founded. As I hung up the phone and began to hastily pack it back in its case, a shadow emerged from behind the door to the stairwell. It came shuffling toward the light of my headlamp. Sandals on tar paper, cheaply woven beige cloth, the smell of tobacco and urine. I pulled my headlamp off so that I wouldn't blind the visitor as I looked up, and discovered with a slight shock that he was already half blind; one eye was a withered socket nestled in a puddle of lax facial muscles. His one good eye seemed equally surprised to discover my blue eyes and pale complexion.

"British?" He squatted down next to me. It was more a statement than a question. I simply nodded and continued packing.

"Bomb?" he asked, pointing at the technology. "No." I directed an uneasy smile in the direction of the good eye and held the numeric pad on the handset up for him to see. "Telephone."

He shook his head. "British bombs no good. Indian bombs no good. Pakistani bombs good."

I nodded again, not in the mood for an esoteric discussion on the merits of explosive devices. On May 28, 1998, less than a month before, Pakistan had successfully detonated a nuclear device in response to India's nuclear tests, becoming the seventh nation on the planet to achieve nuclear power status. Most of the inhabitants of Rawalpindi did not have refrigeration, but the debut of Pakistan on the nuclear stage had done more to boost morale and national pride than a million Frigidares could ever do.

A nuclear arms race between two countries at war with each other did not bode well. Many of the climbers planning expeditions to the western end of the Himalaya had decided to cancel their trips, and the Bulletin of Atomic Scientists had moved the minute hand of the Doomsday Clock, a graphic representation of how close the world is to nuclear armageddon, from 14 to 9 minutes before midnight. Midnight represents nuclear war.

"Jihad," the stranger said suddenly, pointing at the slackness in his cheek.

I stopped packing and looked up. Something about the way he had uttered that single word arrested my attention. So much bitterness, so much longing. Jihad. Holy War. "1975?" I guessed, and he nodded. Another scar in the 50-year-old war against India.

Those who sacrifice their lives in a jihad, *shahids*, die with a promise on their lips. According to Muslim holy men, it is a promise worth dying for: *Janat*, a heavenly paradise in which they will be forgiven for their sins and exist happily ever after in a perfumed camphor garden with beautiful virgin women. Their Indian counterparts on the opposite side of the cease-fire line can only look forward to reincarnation.

But what, I wondered as I looked at the stranger's deformed face, of those whose devotion leads to deformity instead of death? The only thing I had to offer, a handful of rupees in my pocket, might at least fill his stomach. *"Khuda hafiz,"* I smiled and offered the notes from the folds of my garment, hoping the tone of my voice somehow communicated respect. He accepted with a nod.

MORNING AFTER THREE HOURS OF SLEEP WAS A SORDID affair. We sat around, nursing cups of tea and skimming through the newspaper in the lounge of the Shalimar, trying to postpone the inevitable trip out into the midday heat to solve the piton problem.

"Look at this one." I passed the op-ed section over to Zee, pointing at a letter from a Pindi resident. "India aims to prevail upon our society," it read, "first by excelling in the weapons race and secondly by injecting its cultural values into our society by satellite channels. Pakistan's nuclear explosions have boosted our morale. We have decided to break the begging bowl. The world will no longer see us dependent on foreign aid. Now is the time to pay taxes and put all our effort into the development of the country. Work, work, and work is the motto that Quaid-I-Azam wanted us to practice. Now we have decided to follow it. We will work all week long, including Sundays."

Zee let out one of the belly laughs that he was famous for. "Too bad the Minister of Tourism doesn't agree with this guy," he commented. "We might have been able to arrange a Sunday meeting with him."

I nodded. We had all been mildly irritated at having to postpone our departure by a day in order to meet with the minister. It was an inconvenience, but after months of uncertainty about the permit and political events, another 24-hour delay seemed minor. K2 lies on the border of Pakistan and China, a dozen or so miles as the crow flies from active fighting along the Indo-Pakistani border. It is well within the "militarized zone" around Kashmir, so anyone who wishes to climb on the south side of K2 must apply for a permit.

AFTER SEVERAL HOURS OF LUGGING BARRELS FROM ONE room to another, Zee, Chris, and I finally set out from the Shalimar. Noon is a particularly disagreeable time to be out on the streets. Sweat instantly began dripping down the back of my neck, following the curvature of my spine as I half-ran, half-walked, tugging at the edges of the ridiculous pink dopatta, the traditional shawl that I had chosen to wear to avoid panhandlers, trying to keep pace with Zee. His stride was rapid, confident, weaving through spice carts, past a baker fishing roti bread from the black hole of a tandoori oven, around a cluster of squatting children peering at some hidden novelty, a bug perhaps, or a candy wrapper or forked stick. Zee, too, was wearing traditional Pakistani garb: a *kurta*, pajamas, and Balti hat. Whose face, whose body, was this? I wondered as I watched him walk through the streets as though he had lived in Pindi all his life, this partner of mine for the past seven years. The folds of the kurta draped naturally over his angular shoulders, as though his body were made for the garment, instead of the reverse. Maybe it was the nine months of separation, or the heat and the haze, but somehow he seemed more distant, more unfamiliar than ever.

Only his eyes were instantly familiar, etched in the emotions of my past the way a mother's eyes are embedded in the memories of a child. Eyes filled with an opaque brown, the impenetrable brown of turbid jungle tributaries. Those eyes concealed deep eddies of anger, and laughter, and grief, emotions lurking just beneath the surface. Eyes don't change.

The fifth in a family of six children, Zee was five years old when his family emigrated from the Armenian enclave of Kessab, Syria, to the American metropolis of Boston. No birth records were kept in Kessab. His mother remembers falling out of an apple tree during the autumn harvest shortly before his birth, but in the chaos of INS formalities, his appointed date of birth became February 23, 1966. No death records were kept either. A second cousin twice removed came to visit from Kessab a year or so after we were married. "Chuckles," we had called the cousin, a tribute to her dark, hollow cheeks, sagging jowls, and the black holes in her eyes. Back in Kessab, Chuckles had lost her husband and each of her four sons, one by one, to a village well filled with poisonous gasses. "When did it happen?" I wanted to know. "No one knows, and it doesn't matter," was the response.

"Family" was one of the English words Zee's father was particularly fond of. "Family is the only thing that matters." He'd lean back in his armchair after a good meal, patting his belly and ready to lecture any of his brood who would pretend to listen. "You take care of the family, it grows like the garden, and all the rest, it doesn't matter."

When Zee was growing up, the world outside family was considered a desert, an urban world in which he withered and cracked under the taunts and jeers of Irish and Italians and other immigrants more American than he.

I WAS JUST ABOUT TO GIVE UP ON THE QUEST FOR PITONS when Zee stopped, triumphant, in front of the stall of a metallurgist. "There," he declared with a flourish. Inside, a man in a maroon kurta and white cap was crouched on the concrete, carefully hitting a slab of metal with a mallet, working the piece until it fractured and clattered to the floor. His demeanor and rhythmic movements were meditative, almost monastic, the mallet clanging in synch with the sounds of a call to prayer broadcast over the loudspeakers from a nearby mosque.

He had no lathes or drills, no Snap-On tool calendars or power outlets, but I decided to give him a try. I pulled one of our sample pins out of the folds of my garment, and explained that we were looking for someone to make ten of these "pee-tones." He turned it over in his hand a few times, scratched his head, tugged at his white beard, and finally announced, "Ten pee-tones, two weeks."

Zee and I exchanged morose glances. *Two weeks?* The climbing season in the Karakoram is only about ten weeks long. Two weeks would be a serious setback.

"Two days?" I pleaded.

He tugged his beard some more, shook his head, and made a final offer: "Two days, twenty dollars."

We accepted.

EXPEDITIONS GOING TO EVEREST TRADITIONALLY RECEIVE a blessing from a Buddhist monk in a ceremony called a *puja*. There are no Buddhist monks or pujas in Pakistan, but there are palmists.

"Ever been to a palm reader?" I asked Hiddle.

"Yeah." He seemed annoyed by the memory. "One of my cousins brought a palm reader—a friend of hers, I think—to a family reunion once. Some time between the egg toss and the barbecue we all took turns sitting down at a red-and-white-checked picnic bench to get our palms read. *So* quaint. The palm reader was a squishy kind of woman with long wavy blond hair. Not the kind of person you'd expect to have any, you know, astral connections. She told my Uncle Fred that his fate line ended prematurely, which meant that he'd lost his way some time in his 30s or 40s."

"What'd she say about *your* palm?"

Hiddle laughed. "I can't remember," he confessed.

"We went to a palm reader in Rawalpindi," I told him, "I'd never been to one before, but it seemed like a good idea given that we were heading to K2 for two months. You can get this scrambled-eggs sensation when you realize that you are in a black-and-white world that really doesn't give a damn about whether or not you survive. So it seemed like a good idea to have a lodestar to carry us through all the weeks of doubt and anxiety about the weather. I dragged Chris and Zee along, too. Told them Julius Caesar used palm readers to judge his men, and who was I to question Caesar's leadership ability?"

As WE WALKED DOWN THE STREET, AWAY FROM THE PITON maker's shop, it was hard not to feel elated, almost triumphant. Providence was clearly on our side. We had made the commitment to climb K2 nine months prior, and ever since there had been a steady smooth firing of fortuitous coincidences at precisely the right moment, like pistons in an engine.

Even the problem of finding the right palmist and a translator solved itself. At the taxi stand outside the hotel, there was one driver waiting. He happened to have a cousin who was a palmist. He happened to speak English fluently. He happened to be willing to translate for us.

The taxi driver even happened to take a wrong turn on the way, which delayed our arrival by a few minutes, so that we found ourselves climbing the stone stairwell to the palmist's quarters at precisely the moment that the muezzin began to chant the afternoon prayers. It was the reverberation of the prayers in the stairwell that triggered the sense of foreboding, the feeling that we were climbing towards a prophecy. *Get a grip,* I chided myself, but no matter how hard I tried to focus, to climb the stairs steadily and slowly, holding a camera given us to film the expedition on my shoulder, I felt my body swaying with the rhythm of the chanted prayers, my will ebbing away. At the top of the stairs was a sign with a larger-than-life outstretched brown palm, marked with red lines and surrounded by Urdu script, propped in a recess in the stone wall, behind an iron grille cage. The upper left corner was rotting away, I noticed, methodically being consumed by termites and time.

The taxi driver ushered us into a small turquoise room flooded with a neon glare. The room was dominated by a metal desk. Behind it was a tiny man wearing an impossibly white kurta, munching aniseed and drinking from a bottle of Coca-Cola through a straw. *A businessman,* I thought. This was no great palmist, no astrologer or fortuneteller or seer of deep universal secrets.

We stood in front of the desk, shifting from one foot to the other and nervously exchanging glances, waiting for the palmist to finish what appeared to be a long column of calculations. He finally looked up and motioned to Chris to sit down on the bench next to the desk.

I watched Chris squirm as the palm reader scrutinized his hand, pointing at the lines with his pen, turning it around and over. The pen jotted down a string of indecipherable symbols, maybe ancient Vedic scripts or numerals that encoded the drift of the stars. The unlikely soothsayer consulted with his cousin, sitting next to Chris, pointed at the hand again, took more notes.

We waited. More conversation between the taxi driver and his cousin.

"He says," the taxi driver finally intoned in a deep, ponderous voice, "that you have problems with your teeth. You need to brush your teeth more often."

Chris looked over at us with big, earnest round eyes. "Wow, he's right, I do have problems with my teeth." I stifled a laugh.

The palm reader dismissed Chris, and I sat down in his spot, palm outstretched. I had laughed too soon. Was it because I anticipated a cheap circus-tent performance? Whatever it was, it was a palm reading I'll never forget.

THE CAR WAS STOPPED, STUCK BEHIND A TRUCK IN A LINE of traffic that was creeping along behind a plow trying to remove a foot of accumulated snow. I turned the wipers off and crossed my arms across my chest, trying to warm my fingers in my armpits.

"You're not going to believe this," I warned Hiddle, "and I'm not even sure I know how to adequately describe it. The palm reader wouldn't hold my hand, of course, because he was Muslim and I'm female. So I sat there with my palm held out, my elbow propped on my knee, and as he pointed and jotted down symbols, I started to stare at the lines and patterns myself. It was the circular prints on the tip of my middle finger that started to change first. They started to ripple, to undulate like waves spreading in a puddle of water. As I watched the ripples, I felt as if my body, my brain, everything around me, was dilating, expanding to encompass other possible worlds."

There was a vision of the world I was in the process of manifesting, the mother trying to make a living doing what she loved, climbing mountains. In another, I was married but childless, traveling to Pakistan with an unfamiliar husband, wearing five-star clothing and carrying a waistbelt stuffed with rupees and credit cards. There was the lonely single self who loved all God's children and worked for an NGO, teaching English in a village in the Northwestern Territories. There was the professor of mathematics, touring the world during a sabbatical. Each ripple was like a parallel universe, a nest of circular ribbons arcing through time, pinned together at the origin, that necessary moment in time at the palm reader's place in Pindi.

"I think it was the end experience that bothered me more than any single vision. There was this self in an ice cave, a female climber in a yellow suit, peeling off layer after layer of clothing. It was dark, and obviously cold, but she was warm, probably dying of hypothermia. Only I don't think the climber was me. It was a *self*, but it wasn't me."

"Weird," Hiddle said flatly, but he obviously didn't get what I was trying to explain.

I decided to ditch the palm reader topic.

"So we went back to check on the pitons two days later, and discovered that the metallurgist had actually managed to cold-forge ten pitons, complete with the round holes to clip the carabiners through, in two days. It had obviously been an epic for him—he was holding his lower back and kind of limping, as though he had been squatting with an anvil on the floor for all of those 48 hours. We paid him more than 20 bucks, of course."

"Where are they now?" Hiddle asked. "Up on the mountain?"

"No, we managed to recover most of them. I think they're with the rest of my equipment, in my storage shed. Why?"

"No reason," he shrugged, "just curious."

We had both lost interest in the story, maybe because of the monotony of the irregular but predictable rhythm of the traffic. I crept along at 25 miles an hour, turned the wipers on to knock off chunks of slush thrown up on the windshield, gently slid to a stop behind the screeching brakes of the truck in front of us, then started the whole cycle over again.

Why, I wondered, had the image of Wanda appeared in my mind at the palm reader's? It was one of those experiences, like a dream, that slipped away from me as soon as we stepped back out onto the street. I shook my head and dismissed the bizarre experience as a figment of an overactive imagination. Sitting in the car on the highway, though, I knew the vision was real. It was Wanda. Wanda wearing yellow. Wanda dying in a kind of indentation, a cave in the snow somewhere. I shivered and shook my head again, trying to shake off the memory. *That's ridiculous,* the rational part of my brain argued: There are no "caves" in the snow at 8,000 meters, at least none like the one in that vision, only crevasses, and she'd never lie down in a crevasse, of course. The *why?* question still bothered me, though. Why did I have that vision? I had no real reason to care, as far as I knew.

Beware of all enterprises that require new clothes.

—HENRY DAVID THOREAU,
Walden

TELL THEM IT'S MY RELIGION

I started talking again, anxious to think about something else.

"From Pindi," I told him, "you have a 30-hour bus ride on an infamous section of the Old Silk Road known as the Karakoram Highway to get to a place called Skardu. *Bus* and *highway* are misnomers, though."

The Karakoram "Highway" is actually a narrow road that winds through the debris of a geological collision zone formed by four of the world's highest mountain ranges—the Himalaya, the Karakoram, the Hindu Kush, and the Pamir. It is one of those remarkable engineering feats, like Stonehenge or the Sphinx, that must have required intense physical labor and human sacrifice.

Riding along this engineering feat is not for travelers with weak hearts or weak bladders. A rainstorm along certain sections of the highway can trigger massive landslides that can take days to clear, so when the weather is good, drivers will typically work for up to four days without sleep, driving for stretches of six hours or more without stopping.

Under the best of conditions, many sections of the road, particularly the one running from Sasli to Skardu, would be a challenge for an expert off-road driver in a rugged four-wheel-drive vehicle. The vehicle of choice, the traditional hand-painted Pakistani bus that I like to call a *junga*, is more like a garbage truck than a 4x4. Anybody who has ever traveled in one of these vehicles will never forget it. They are regularly exploding, losing the steering or other vital functions, and running off precipitous cliffs. The drivers are a wild-eyed breed of fanatics who pride themselves in expertly executing heart-stopping horn-blaring charges at oncoming vehicles, protected of course by the prayers to Allah that adorn the ornately painted interior and exterior of the bus.

Hiddle was clearly anticipating a good tale, so I decided to tell him about the bus that caught fire on the trip to GII.

THERE WERE SIX OF US INSIDE THE VEHICLE, CLIMBERS AND trekkers on the 1996 GII expedition traveling from Pindi to Skardu, and the thick black smoke must have been spewing out from the back of the bus for about 15 minutes before we decided it was something worth shouting about.

"Fire! *Fuego! Feu!* Stop the bus!" We writhed on our bellies across the sea of barrels and duffel bags piled inside the bus, trying to worm our way to the front. The Pakistani driver and his mate in the cab were oblivious to our panic, intent on performing yet another maniacal swerve around a hairpin bend 500 feet above the churning Indus River.

Someone finally threw an empty water bottle into the cab to get the driver's attention. He glanced in the mirror, grinned, cocked his head, and swept his hand through the air in a half-crazed gesture that was both magnanimous and apologetic.

"No problem. Just a leetle smoke. Is O.K.!"

He hadn't slept in at least two days. He had been driving our bus for more than 20 hours, fueled by "wacky-backy" cigarettes, a fresh batch of hashish drying on the dashboard, and the high-pitched desirous whining of a female singing in Urdu. We had already experienced a brake-system failure and a flat tire on our other bus. Now this one was on fire, and somehow we needed to convince him that pulling over would be a good idea.

Risk and real danger are important elements of high-altitude climbing, but I hadn't reckoned on this sort of hazard. Sure, I knew there would be avalanches and crevasses on the mountain. But there is a huge difference between risking your life at the hands of a wannabe race car driver and willingly putting your life at the mercy of the whims of nature.

The thick black smoke from the oil fire finally reached the cab and the driver's nostrils, and the bus lurched to the side of the road. "Deener time," he announced, staggering out and disappearing into one of the hovels by the road. We tumbled out and ran to the opposite side of the road, half expecting the bus with our 100 canisters of fuel and other expedition gear to explode in a Hollywood-style inferno. It didn't.

And so, after half an hour of vainly trying to find the source of the fire, we, too, shrugged and went into the dirt-floor restaurant. The only item on the menu was hunks of meat that we christened

"Death in a Bowl," served with the standard fare of chappatis and dal. When the bus driver emerged from the kitchen to inspect our appetites, he confirmed that the dish was everything we imagined.

"Is this cow?" I asked, jabbing the contents of the bowl with my fork.

"Cow? Ah, cow. Yez, yez. Is cow."

"Is it the entrails?" a more sophisticated teammate chimed in.

"En-tray-ahls?" the bus driver repeated, looking even more puzzled, "Yez, yez."

"Is it... roadkill?" I ventured.

"Roadkill! Yez, yez. Veti good roadkill." This time he nodded vigorously. "Eat!" He pointed impatiently at the bowl and then at me.

Unable to come up with a graceful excuse, I obliged and fed a forkful of roadkill to an unwilling gut. As we piled back into the bus, I felt the meat's bacteria take hold of my lower intestine with a sudden lurch. "How," I groaned to myself, "am I gonna make it through another ten-hour ride to the next pit stop?"

HIDDLE WAS LAUGHING HARD AS I PAUSED. "OH, MAN," he grinned, "why the hell'd you eat the stuff?"

"I told, you, I couldn't come up with a good reason not to," I said defensively, "You get so used to ingesting weird bacteria anyhow, it's hard to know which meal your gut can handle, and which meal will leave your stomach so twisted that you have to sleep squatting over a hole."

Actually, several weeks after the Death in a Bowl meal—a few weeks too late—I did come up with a one-liner that would have been a culturally acceptable way of declining the bus driver's invitation.

I was standing next to a stream just below the Baltoro glacier, watching a Balti porter deftly rinse a freshly killed goat gut in the water. Normally I try to refrain from making cultural judgments, but in this particular case, it seemed unavoidable. There was no way I could stand and blithely watch the guy pollute the only source of potable water in the entire valley with the green, foul-smelling intestines of a goat. Contaminating the stream was wrong. Some truths are universal.

So I cleared my throat and squatted down next to him. "You shouldn't clean the goat here. It will make the water dirty," I announced, pointing at the water.

He looked at me incredulously. The water was already dirty with glacial silt.

"The goat's stomach has germs. Germs in the water will make us sick."

With the language barrier, the porter finally latched on to the two English words I kept using: "bacteria" and "germs."

"Bacteria...part of science, no?" he queried.

"Yes!" I smiled, nodding encouragement, "Science. Bacteria, germs, bad."

"No, no problem, no problem," he laughed, shaking his head and looking relieved. "Science *your* religion, not mine."

Religion, you see, is a supremely powerful word, one capable of excusing no end of odd behavior.

When the bus driver commanded "Eat!" I should have simply shook my head and said, "Roadkill *your* religion, not mine."

"SO WHAT HAPPENED ON THE K2 EXPEDITION?" HIDDLE asked after I was silent for a few minutes.

"You mean on the Karakoram Highway?"

He nodded.

"Well, we got to choose the driver and the bus, so we didn't have engine problems, but we were still detained for about eight hours at a roadblock."

ANXIOUS TO AVOID A REPEAT OF THE BUS-ON-FIRE SCENARIO, I decided that one of my jobs as leader of the K2 expedition would be to hand-pick a junga bus in Islamabad. That entails a trip to the bus yard, an idea that was not met with enthusiasm by the agent organizing our trip, a Pakistani climber named Ashraf Aman. "I will go myself to choose a bus for you," he generously offered. "There are many very modern buses. I can get a good bus from the Masherbrum company with air conditioning and soft seats. The Masherbrum bus is better than the buses you call jungas."

Air conditioning? No, no, no. I had already seen a few Masherbrum buses lumbering around town. There were no roll bars on the outside, so we wouldn't be able to climb like monkeys all over the bus while it was moving. Sleeping can be a problem on a junga bus, but I figured we could make a sort of mattress by piling the barrels and duffel bags up above the level of the seats in the back half of the bus. So what if neither the bags nor the bus had springs. The ride was only 30 hours anyway, and the sleep deprivation wasn't bad training for the summit bid.

Ashraf finally yielded to my stubbornness and commissioned Issa Khan, his brother-in-law, to drive us to the bus yard. There we learned that many of the junga-style buses were built with engines made by a company called Bedford, which had gone out of business. Parts had been unavailable for a year or two, and the mechanics for many of the buses were the drivers themselves. When we asked one driver how he repaired his bus without Bedford parts, he grinned and produced a sledgehammer.

That made the elimination part of the selection process easier. No buses with Bedford engines. No buses with charred frames or other signs of uncontrolled combustion. No buses with bald tires (tires from Britain with less than a two-millimeter tread are often exported to Pakistan, where there is no minimum tread requirement). No buses too tall to fit under the overhanging cliffs along the road. No buses with engines covered in oil. No buses with wacky-backy drivers.

Actually, selecting a bus was a little more difficult, but we finally settled on a bus with a Nissan diesel engine and two very docile-looking drivers. One of the artists at the bus yard, a guy with a kurta covered with splotches of paint and a portable pallet of colors, was just putting the final touches on another prayer to Allah at the back of the bus.

Both of the drivers, I was told, were devout Muslims who liked to stop to pray five times per day. This seemed like a match made in heaven, because I like to stop to pee five times per day.

And so we set out for what I assumed would be a relatively uneventful trip to Skardu.

No such luck. Twenty-seven hours and five stops from Islamabad, the bus came to a grinding halt. Three hundred very angry men from the village of Taloo, in the Dhrundoo region, had erected a barrier of rocks and stones in the middle of the road to protest the education commissioner's failure to send a village teacher. There were no phones in the village. The commissioner lived 300 miles away. It looked like a long wait.

It was.

Six hours later, when no one had even been dispatched to summon the commissioner because the protesters had threatened to stone the messenger, I decided to attempt a dialogue with the village chief.

There was one small problem. The liaison officer who had been assigned to our expedition, a Pakistani army captain, adamantly refused even to let me out of the bus.

We had a satellite phone, I argued. If I could get out to talk to the village leader, maybe I could persuade him to use our phone to call the commissioner.

"No," the captain said firmly, "I cannot let you go out there. You see? It is all angry men. There is no woman. They will raise sticks to you."

The beginnings of a bad idea were dawning in my mind. "Would a Shiite Muslim man," I asked slowly, "ever raise a stick to a *pregnant* woman?"

"Not if she is married," he answered, absently staring out the window, oblivious to the hidden intent in the question.

I eagerly clambered into the back of the bus, ducked behind a pile of barrels, stripped my clothes off, and emerged two minutes later in a very convincing six-months pregnant condition with a wad of clothes carefully bunched and smoothed out under a baggy shalwar kameez. The captain hooted with laughter, and I climbed out of the bus before he could object.

My plan backfired. Outside, in the dust and the heat, our Pakistani guide, Jahn, was surrounded by a cluster of angry, gesturing men. I walked toward him, feeling very conspicuous and a little bit foolish. I was the only woman in sight, dressed in bright pink swaths of fabric. Looking very pregnant.

Before I could reach the village chief, I was intercepted by Jahn. He put his arm around my shoulders in a protective gesture and firmly guided me back to the bus, shaking his head. Inside, he collapsed in a fit of laughter, covering his face with his hands. "What are you doing? I just told them you are the 1998 American K2 expedition leader," he groaned. "Now they want to know why a woman in this—this *state*"—he gestured to my belly—"is going to climb K2!"

It was my turn to laugh. This was the most interesting variation on the "why climb K2?" question I had ever encountered. "Tell them we're doing a scientific study of the effects of altitude on childbirth," I suggested. Then I remembered the conversation I had had with the goat-guts guy two years before. "No, better yet," I decided, "don't try to use the word science. Just tell them it's my *religion*."

Himalayan climbing could not exist without danger. Without risk there would be no adventure. That, I believe, is what gives it its worth.

—Maurice Herzog

FELINE THINGS

"Rest stop a quarter mile ahead," Hiddle said. "Mind pulling in?"
I had the vague feeling that there was something more I wanted to say about the roadblock and Zee's reaction to it, some part of the eight-hour wait in the heat and the way it had affected our relationship, but I veered off the highway and into a rest area parking lot anyhow. The silence after the engine shuddered to a stop was deafening. I yawned, stretched, and realized I needed to be alone for a few minutes.

"Go ahead on in," I told Hiddle, tipping the seat back. "I'll be there in a few."

He looked at me dubiously and then nodded quickly and disappeared.

The tubular glare of a white neon light in the parking lot revealed sheets of snow being driven sideways by the wind. I stared glassy-eyed at the flakes landing and sliding down through the mush on the windshield. I tried to tune out the vaguely annoying sounds of pneumatic truck brakes and revving engines and then finally gave up and trudged through the snow and slush to the rest-stop bathroom in a thoroughly grumpy mood.

When I emerged, Hiddle was leaning against the car, legs crossed, blowing a thin puff of smoke toward the clouds. I noticed his hair for the first time, long and flecked with gray, pinned at the nape of his neck, with a bizarre white skunk streak running back from the center of his forehead.

I was about to make some comment about the smoking and then realized that he probably assumed that I was a smoker, too. When I had bought the car from the refuse manager at a recycling center in New Hampshire, it had smelled like a $500 ashtray. I had added incense, charcoal, baking soda, air fresheners, potpourri, and a special kind of baby cedar boughs that someone saw on a Home & Garden show. Now it smelled like a $550 pine-and-lemon ashtray.

We reluctantly crammed our bodies back into a sitting position and edged back onto the highway, wipers flipping full blast.

"You must have a pretty extensive family if you've got enough people to have reunions," I remarked. I had completely lost track of the K2 saga and wasn't really in the mood to talk about the Himalaya anyhow.

"Yeah, I've got 13 uncles and a bevy of cousins. No immediate family, though. No sibs, and my folks died in a plane accident a few years ago."

"So you live alone?" He finally seemed in an open enough mood to field a few biographical questions.

"Well, yeah, I guess so. Not exactly *alone,* though. I'm a wildlife photographer, so I usually have an animal of some kind living with me, depending on where my next shoot is. I get them from a friend of mine who's an exotic pet guy. He'll loan me a croc, or a boa, or a kangaroo, or a cheetah, whatever he has. It'd be kind of hard to find someone to live with," he added with a laugh, "when you've got a different dangerous pet every few months."

"You *live* with the animals you're going to photograph?" I asked incredulously, trying to gauge whether he was telling the truth. As soon as I said it, of course, I felt like an idiot. Who was I to question this guy when I had just spun out a string of what must have sounded like improbable stories about climbing in the Himalaya? At least being a wildlife photographer explained why he was so comfortable with listening to stories about other countries.

"Just the baby ones," he responded, unfazed by my skepticism. "You can learn a lot about the way a thing thinks in the wild by watching the way it acts in captivity. I came home one day and this cheetah cub had reached through the bars of his cage and shredded a pillow that had fallen off my bed. He was pouncing on the feathers like mice. So when I went to Botswana, I took a sack of feathers and got some really amazing cub shots. You've just got to know how the feline mind works."

Déjà vu, I thought. This was at least the third or fourth time somebody had tried to tell me that the key to understanding big cats was knowing small cats. I still didn't get the point.

"You really think that's all there is to it?" I asked him, "I mean, I've always felt like cougars and tigers and that kind of thing are more than just big kitty cats. I used to live in Oregon, and when I was running up in the hills I'd see deep prints on the trails, or a shadow moving along the top of a ridge, or the cougar itself. Somehow I was always *aware*, if I stopped running and panting for a minute, if there was a cougar nearby. I've never felt that kind of awareness with an ordinary cat."

ON ONE PARTICULAR RUN I HEARD A SMALL CREATURE DIE as I emerged from a stand of trees at the edge of a meadow.

It started out like any other early morning run in the Oregon coastal range. I probably stretched for a few minutes, trying to coax my mind and body from the womb of the night. Cracked my toe knuckles, gave my shoelaces the ritual tugs. Grabbed a few clumsy gulps of water at the kitchen faucet, head tipped sideways, and wiped the cheek dribble off on the back of a mitten. Silently opened the front door and stepped out, into the darkness.

There's something primitive about the ritual of running in the hills before dawn. The itchy, sweaty hair under the band of the headlamp on your forehead. The white circle of light bobbing up and down. The gnarled roots, rocks, and branches on the trail that make every step a dance with the chaotic patterns of nature. Sometimes I'd stop in the middle of a dense, dark area and turn the headlamp off. You can't run without it, but you can stand with wide eyes blind in the dark and feel the rhythmic pounding of your heart making waves in the blackness around you.

You learn to trust the darkness, despite the fear that it triggers.

I reached the meadow just before dawn—that hour of the morning when a few stars still dance in the sky and the whole world waits without breathing for the first wave of light. The long, wet grassy weeds at the edge of the narrow path licked my legs in rhythmic swishes, but I felt something unusual in the clearing that morning.

A sudden pulse of tingling electricity ran down the back of my neck. At the edge of the meadow was a dark shape, crouched and twitching.

Before I had time to think, the shape shattered the silence with a high-pitched scream.

A cougar, throttling its prey.

The tingling ran down to my fingertips, and I stopped, held my breath, and squatted down. Turned my headlamp off. Crept a little closer. Probably not a wise thing to do. Not a sign of Darwinian maturity. But some deep instinct within me wanted to see the source of that piercing scream, to witness the struggle, the raw life energy being transferred from one creature to another. As my eyes adjusted, I could see the black outlined form of the cat and the bushy tail of its victim, probably a squirrel. A low growl suddenly warned me not to come closer, and I froze, a wannabe wild creature balancing precariously on all fours, tearing the skin of my jacket on thorns hidden in the dewy undergrowth.

Two eyes, two spots of yellow fire, emerged unblinking from the black form, and my instincts suddenly flailed. There was something in those feral, glowing spots I didn't understand, something full of a deep, defiant, and untamable sort of comprehension. Something, I suppose, that allows cougars to calmly inhabit their lives.

We have no problem feeling a sappy affinity with the natural world, with trees and wildflowers and sunsets, until we confront the truly wild parts of it, the cougars and avalanches and rattlesnakes that challenge our ability to confront death without whimpering, to accept the inevitable. In the presence of the wild, attempting to see beauty, to grasp the meaning of the experience is a little like trying to drink from a fire hydrant.

As I crouched in the meadow gaping at the cougar, that condition of the brain we call reason returned. The Oregon state legislature had passed a ban on hunting cougars that year, and with the hearty recovery of the population, the media had published a series of speculative articles designed to satisfy the public appetite for virtual fear. Cougars are cats, the media explained, so they typically hunt during the waning of the night for animals that run and twitch and move furtively.

"Running in the hills before dawn is a bad idea because you're about the same size as a healthy deer," one cautious friend had warned me.

"Avoid wearing catnip perfume," another helpful friend had recommended.

Climb a tree if you are threatened, an article in the local paper had advised.

I stood up and slowly backed away, holding my headlamp high above my head and shining it on the trees several feet above the cougar's head, hoping that the rumors I had heard about wild cats being easily impressed by height were true.

Half an hour later, after an interminable series of switchbacks and nervous backward glances, I reached the usual turnaround point, a clearing at the crest of a hill. I flopped one foot up onto a stump to stretch and enjoy the view. In the east, the horizon was erupting in bands of color. In the west, the usual bank of fog was retreating, peeling back to the vast open expanses of the distant

Pacific, exposing the endless rolling blue waves of the coastal hills. And from somewhere in the recesses of my memory, the experiences of the morning dredged up the sound of monks chanting during the hour of the monastic vigils, that beautiful, rhythmic celebration of the fears of the night, the mystery of silence and vacant time.

"HOUSE CATS AREN'T HUMAN PREDATORS." HIDDLE BROUGHT me back to our conversation with a reminder of the obvious. "So, yeah, of course you're not going to feel *fear* around them. They're all part of the same species, though."

I could sense the conversation was getting combative, and, with a suddenly much fuller picture of the guy in the seat next to me, I decided it'd be better to go in another direction. "So if you've been living around all these animals to get in tune with their inner nature, which kind of animal do you identify with? You know, which creature would you choose to be?"

"Bear," he answered without hesitation. "I've never bunked with a bear, but they've got this very admirable streak of laziness and efficiency, this way of lumbering and lolling around and then casually killing whatever will give them the most energy for the least amount of effort. I spent some time in South Korea last year, trying to find Asiatic black bears, these Tibetan moon bears that have a crescent-shaped mark of dirty yellow fur down under their paunch. It's amazing how difficult it is to get near bears in Korea. They're all gun shy because there's so much poaching. Bear paws are a delicacy. I think the gall bladders are worth *bhats*, too."

"Why?" he added. "What's your alter animal ego?"

"Oh, I don't know." I shrugged the question off. "A yeti, maybe. They're supposed to smell really bad, and I can identify with that."

Hiddle smiled but didn't let me off the hook, "No, it's got to be an animal that's been photographed."

"Probably a tiger."

"I thought so," he nodded.

"What do you mean, you *thought so*?" I demanded. "Are you trying to tell me I have feline proclivities or something?"

"No," he laughed. "You didn't look anything like a cat stumbling through the snow at the rest stop back there. I was just thinking of a Korean myth that a guide from Seoul told me while we were out in the hills. There's a bear and a tiger living in a cave, praying to a mountain god—Hwanung, I think—to turn them into humans. So Hwanung gives them a bundle of mugworts and a hundred cloves of garlic and tells them to stay in the cave and eat them, to resist the lure of the sunlight outside, for 100 days. The bear succeeds, is transformed into a woman, and gives birth to a son named Tan'gun Wanggom, who is supposed to have ruled a country called Choson for 1,500 years until he eventually became a mountain god himself at the ripe old age of 1,908. The tiger remains a tiger."

I thought for a moment. "But why'd the tiger fail? Because he didn't like garlic, or because he couldn't resist the lure of the sunlight?"

"I don't know. You'd probably be able to answer that question better than I would."

I ignored his attempt to rile me. "And what's a mugwort, anyway?"

"An herb."

"Yeah, I guessed that much. Do you know what it's used for?"

"Mmm, I think you can put it in a bath to bring on menstruation. Or you can squeeze it and use the juice as an antidote to opium. Or you can dry it and sleep on a pillow full of it to experience dreams about love and your future. You can stick a leaf up your nose, too, to cure a headache."

"All right, all right," I conceded, laughing. "I'm sorry I asked."

*When you pass through, no one can pin you
down, no one can call you back.*

—YING-AN

KANCH AVALANCHE

"**S**o you're the Bear who, with patience and perseverance, gets what he wants, and you think I'm the Tiger who can't resist the lure of the sunshine?" I couldn't just let Hiddle off the hook so easily. I actually wanted to push the conversation further. I was intrigued by the myth.

He didn't say anything.

I decided to probe anyway. "Tigers as a metaphor do have a reputation for being free spirits. Cats are restless and aloof and autonomous, and I guess those particular adjectives would describe me—or most of the women who have climbed in the Himalaya, for that matter. It's almost impossible to maintain any normal domestic relationships when you're gone for months at a time, and as a woman in a male-dominated sport, you have to be independent in order to survive. I wouldn't be surprised if most of the female Himalayan climbers identified with snow leopards or Siberian tigers. Alison Hargreaves, for example. She was one of those three women I told you about on K2, one of the three who made it to the top but didn't survive the descent. I know she was fond of the Tibetan saying: 'It's better to live one year as a tiger than a thousand years as a sheep.'

"The sunlight element is even more interesting, though. I've always identified the urge to climb mountains with the lure of the moon, the reflected sunlight, that *luna dementia* that waxes each month with the dilation of the moon. What is it that is so appealing about an orb of light in the sky?" I mused. "You can't look at the sun directly—it is too intense. Is the moon is a paradigm for the fascination with the life energy that we receive from the sun?

"Or is there some primeval appeal in a circle of light? Some dim collective memory of a luminescent globe, a sunburst at the end of a tunnel?"

Hiddle's telling of the Korean myth had unleashed a cascade of ideas. My thoughts were tumbling over one another, little rivulets of insight merging to form a sudden cataract of comprehension. The moon, the moths, the avalanche, the lama and the labyrinth, the tiger, the postcard, even the taillights of the car in front of me, like red blood cells moving unsteadily through a clotted universe; somehow it all made sense.

I wasn't sure where to start.

"There was this light," I was fishing for the right words, "this *light* that radiated out, sort of like the sun, in this avalanche that I was caught in on Kanchenjunga."

Hiddle was listening attentively, but I realized he had no idea what I was talking about.

"Kanchenjunga, or just 'Kanch' for short, is another one of the big Himalayan peaks," I explained. "It's the third highest mountain in the world, after Everest and K2, and it's a mountain that the Tibetan Buddhists consider holy—the most holy of the 8,000-meter peaks. It's really huge, somehow much bigger than Everest or K2. I guess you could call it the biggest massif in the world. 'Kanch' means five in Nepali, and it has five summits, four of which are above 8,000 meters. Five summits, five 'treasures of the snow.' Each represents something different, like the five colors in the prayer flags. And the ridges of the mountain are aligned more or less in a north-south-east-west pattern, which makes it even more sacred, although I don't know how the Tibetan monks around the mountain know that, because you'd really have to have an aerial view of the mountain to realize it."

Yes, the avalanche on Kanchenjunga was the place to start. I felt nauseous again as soon as I thought about it.

THE LOUD *CRACK* AND THE CRESCENDO OF THUNDERING snow above me flooded my mind with a numbness colder than the white wave that was about to wash over me. I swung each axe, sinking them as deep as I could into the hard green ice, and ran through a series of cool calculations. I was alone in a steep, narrow couloir on the north face of Kanchenjunga at about 21,000 feet. With a labyrinth of unstable ice towers on my right and a steep band of rock sweeping up to the left, there was no way to climb to safety, nothing to protect me from the onslaught of snow and ice. Other climbers might hear the roar, but they would hardly pay attention. Avalanches poured down the flank of the mountain every day. Even if anyone noticed the distant rumble, I couldn't expect help. The nearest climber was at least seven hours away, and the difference between survival and stillness is at most seven minutes.

The wave was almost upon me. My mind raced as I hunched over my axes. One of the classic textbooks on mountain climbing, *Mountaineering: The Freedom of the Hills*, instructs climbers to try to swim when caught in an avalanche: "Fight to keep on the surface, swimming on your back with head uphill, flailing arms and legs." *Swim?* With a heavy pack, two ice axes, and crampons? The authors must have been very proficient swimmers. The last thought I had before the wave hit was a vision of training for a Himalayan climb by trying to swim with two ice axes and a pack on in an indoor pool.

Pain ripped through my forehead and my shoulder as the first chunks of ice rained down. Another heavy blow on my pack wrenched me from my tenuous holds, and then the snow engulfed me. After a short slide and several clumsy back flips, I landed face down with tons of wet snow on top of me. I felt my chest collapse, heard air and a groan squeezed from my body. Open mouth, open eyes staring into blackness. The knot of panic in my stomach bubbled up to my throat, and my mind sent desperate, urgent messages to my arms and legs, but they responded only with a dull oxygenless ache. Above me I felt the weight shifting, churning, crushing. As the snow compacted around me, strangely comfortable and warm, like a heavy quilted eiderdown, I slowly relaxed and listened to the continuous low roar of the white wave in a distant, disembodied way. My ears were ringing, and a hot ball of pain pulsed somewhere inside my head. From within it came a voice, calm but insistent: *Roll over.*

Roll over. Move. I struggled, but again nothing happened. Another low rumble, an ache and a flash of light in my eyes, and then suddenly my body began to spin in the darkness. Somewhere in the black depths of the snow I heard an absurd, high-pitched, happy tinkling sound. Carnival music? I was lying on my belly on a warm beach, with my hands and feet buried deep in the hot sand, and in front of me, where the water should be, the darkness had given way to a bright white circle of light.

I don't know how much time passed. The white light was sharp, bright, full of a placid certainty. My mind journeyed slowly toward it, floating through a tunnel, with space and light flowing in straight lines to a single point, flying through a strong magnetic field. The light was like a magnet, my mind like iron filings of awareness focused unambiguously, peacefully, in a single direction.

Blue shadows were moving in slow motion through the light— shadows that sent out waves of electrical energy, waves that washed like walls of awareness through me, flooding my mind with visions of vaguely familiar events that seemed to be happening at points in the future. Each vision seemed to be a juncture, an ephemeral glimpse of some possible reality. The last wave was the most vivid: an aerial image of the mountain, Kanchenjunga. The mountain was a labyrinth, a labyrinth disgorging a child. Somehow I became the labyrinth, and the child fell, as if falling through space, in a streak of light, like a meteor. In a single desperate effort I tried to catch the child, and both the image and the circle of light suddenly exploded in strobes of pain as I reentered my body. The weight of snow on my lungs had been replaced by thin air, and my chest began to spasm and heave.

I rolled in the snow, retching and gagging, fighting for air and expelling frothy pink snow. My mouth, nostrils, ears, goggles, pockets: every orifice was filled with packed snow. The first deep breaths seared my lungs like hot smoke and my head reeled in protest with the rush of cold air. Not until I tore off my goggles and the blinding glare of the snow and storm assaulted my eyes did I realize it with a sudden shock: I was alive.

Alive. Somehow my oxygen-starved limbs had wrenched themselves free, or, more likely, another wave had rolled my body farther down the slope, releasing me from the weight of the snow and ice. I rolled weakly onto my back, ignoring the sharp burn that shot down my arm, the warm trickle of blood on my forehead, the throbbing in my ears, and laughed. The amazed chuckle of an eccentric scientist in the lab. The laugh triggered another paroxysm of coughing and retching, and when it had passed, I rolled over again, alternately laughing and sobbing, squinting up at the sky through wet eyelashes, feeling the cold snowflakes melting in the hot tears on my face.

Returning to the world of the living after the avalanche was like going back to school after a vacation. As I lay in the snow and let the delicious sensations of cold, wet, hot and pain wash through my body, my mind balked at the incongruity of the two worlds I had just experienced. It dallied in the world I had just left, trying to remember the details of the blue shadows that had moved through the circle of light toward me. The hiss of another wave of spindrift sliding down the couloir rudely interrupted my reverie, and I sat up abruptly. *Get out of the couloir, quick.* My shoulder hurt, but I could move it. My ear throbbed, but the pain was bearable. The only real nuisance was the trickle of blood that was dripping down into my right eye from the sticky mat of hair on my forehead. I was carrying an extra 150 feet of rope to Camp 3 instead of little luxuries like a first aid kit, a toothbrush, or extra clothing. There was nothing disposable in my pack that I could tie around my head to stem the bleeding, so I pressed my forehead into the snow, retrieved my ice axes, and slowly picked my way back down the slope.

Twenty minutes away there was a cluster of Korean tents, and as I approached the camp a small chunk of ice that interrupted the smooth downhill flow of the snow caught my eye. I jabbed it with my pole and discovered a *khata*, one of the consecrated white scarves that Buddhist monks sometimes give to climbers for good luck. Finding a white scarf lying in white snow in the flat white light of a storm seemed fortuitous, so I tied it around my forehead and decided to rest.

Exhaustion and shock must have gripped my mind and body. I didn't bother to melt snow or change my wet clothes, and as soon as I crawled into my sleeping bag I slipped into a deep, dreamless sleep that lasted almost 14 hours. When I woke the next morning in a fog, confused and dehydrated, the contrast with the day before was unnerving. In the chute that had almost become my coffin there was no trace of my struggle. No doubt another avalanche had swept it clean, and now it curved in a smooth, innocuous arc up to the crest of the seracs, an easy 600 feet of 60-degree snow and ice. I hesitated, sat for more than an hour staring vacantly at the seracs from the safety of the tent, mesmerized by the silence, the shimmering waves of heat floating above the snow, and the towering blocks of ice stacked in a precarious 1,000-foot-high pile. The slopes were still heavy with unconsolidated snow, the seracs were still unstable, and I was still alone. The nasty little scratch on my forehead was still oozing and my left ear was still throbbing.

I knew that the rational decision was to return to Base Camp to recover, but somehow I couldn't bring myself to go down. Climbing—like survival—is an instinct, a reflex. Every fiber in my body wanted to go up.

AFTER ANOTHER THREE DAYS OF BATTLING THE CONSTANT accumulation of snow from the spindrift pouring down the face onto Camp 2, I finally found myself climbing from Camp 3 to 4 for a summit bid with a teammate named Scott McKee. The weather was perfect, our movements were sure, and we were climbing for the sheer joy of movement. At 25,000 feet, Scott scrambled up to the top of a 10-foot boulder that was perched like a stray meteorite in the middle of a wide terrace. He threw his arms and axes up into the air in a V. Victory over a boulder problem at almost 26,000 feet. I laughed at his recklessness, threw back my head, and howled. We were exhilarated by the view of the glacier snaking like a river 10,000 feet below us, the sea of peaks around us, and the new moon hanging in the deep blue sky over the white horizon above us.

We spent the last three hours of daylight chipping out a tent platform with a Slovak climber and then crawled into the tent. Scott announced that it was his 37th birthday. I tried to make a candle out of our last Power Bar. We drank hot apple cider and toasted the spirit of the mountain. We were still exuberant and strong, only 2,000 feet below the summit, certain that we would reach it.

Several hours later, after we struggled to sleep on the tiny, roughly hewn tent platform in hurricane-force winds, the exuberance and some of our strength had dissipated. We awoke at 2:30, fumbled with the cold stove, pulled on our boots and crampons with wooden fingers, and finally stumbled out of the tent at 5:30.

Plumes of spindrift curled over the summit ridge, and as we inched slowly up the slope, blasts of snow and ice swept across the face, forcing us to hunch over our axes to cover unprotected skin. Two steps, breathe, hunch, blast; five steps, breathe…We were climbing without bottled oxygen in the interest of "style," and finding the energy for each step was difficult. If we had been able to establish a rhythm it might have been more bearable, but the gusts came at irregular, chaotic intervals.

Stop fighting. I wanted to find the wild pulse of the windstorm, to move with the surges of flying ice and snow, to breathe in deeply the thin air. I paused to listen, but the ebb and flow of the wind was unpredictable, and I found myself stumbling, sprinting in between each blast to warm my frozen hands and feet.

Above us the low roar of the jet stream and a 50-mile-long wind plume trailing from the summit signaled impossible conditions on the final ridge leading to the summit. The jet stream moves at speeds in excess of a hundred miles per hour, and a climber on the exposed ridge would have been blown clear into Tibet.

"We'll never make it. Let's save our strength for tomorrow," I shouted, piercing the wind and our high-altitude stupor. I saw Scott nod, and we turned and stumbled back down toward our bivouac.

Back in the tent, we crawled into stiff bags and nursed numb fingers and toes. The bottles of water we had carried next to our bodies inside our down suits were useless cylinders of ice.

"Think we should go down?" Scott asked casually.

"No way." It was my ninth consecutive day on the mountain, and my seventh day above 20,000 feet. I had been strafed by a falling serac, buried by an avalanche. The impact of the avalanche had perforated my eardrum, and I had endured 72 hours of pain and continuous shoveling alone after the avalanche, in a wind storm at Camp 2. I knew that our bodies could succumb to the inevitable effects of altitude exposure at any time, but I wanted to give the wind one more chance to lift.

Later that morning, Scott announced on the radio, "Heidi wants to give it another go, so, against my better judgment, we'll stay up here one more night." I looked at him and laughed. Judgment? What's that? Strange things happen to your brain when oxygen is in short supply. The longer you hang out in the death zone, the more disconnected and incoherent your thoughts become. I had already been troubled for days at Base Camp by vivid hallucinations of leeches on my tent.

We weren't plagued by hallucinations or bizarre high-altitude dreams that particular night, but the wind was even more intense. Melting snow on the hanging stove became a four-hand job, and shards of wind-blown ice tore into our single-wall tent like shrapnel, leaving fist-sized holes that sucked in spindrift. Somewhere in the night I woke with a dull ache in the back of my skull—not from the decreased pressure and lack of oxygen, but from the tent wall slamming into my head each time the wind hit us broadside with the force of a freight train.

When we awoke to begin the routine of melting snow again, things were even worse. The water bottles that we had kept inside our down suits, inside our down sleeping bags, next to our bodies, were frozen, and Scott was partially blind from retinal hemorrhages in one eye.

EIGHTEEN HOURS LATER WE WERE RELAXING IN THE MESS tent at Base Camp. A retinal hemorrhage is a nasty side effect of high altitude that can worsen quickly and cause serious problems on the descent. With this in mind—and with visions of enormous helpings of our cook Songay's specialty, deep-fried potatoes—we had descended quickly, from 26,000 feet to 17,000 feet in a single day.

That night there was a party in the mess tent of the British military expedition. Two of the climbers were talking about Alison Hargreaves, the famous British alpinist who became the first female to solo Everest without supplemental oxygen in 1995 and then died three months later on K2. Frustrated by a season of unusually bad weather, she had decided to stay late in the season to make one last attempt.

She and her partner, Rob Slater, had reached the summit in deteriorating weather, and they had been blown off the mountain during their descent in a typical high-altitude storm. I had climbed with one of Alison's K2 partners on GII in 1996, so I already knew her story, but something in the tone of this particular conversation made me pause.

Both Alison and Rob, these two climbers felt, had been blinded by their "reckless enthusiasm." Rob had even adopted the motto, "Summit or plummet." Despite his retinal hemorrhage, Scott still wanted to give the summit another go. I had planned on joining him, but now I reevaluated the situation. We were already beyond the normal dates for a "weather window" in eastern Nepal, and by the time we were rested and ready to go back up—May 22 or 23—it would be "late in the season."

All of the other expeditions at Base Camp were preparing to leave, and at dinner our cook had announced, "Monsoon weather here." I impulsively decided to leave. The jet stream had been relentlessly scouring the upper reaches of the mountain for over a month, and not one of the 37 climbers on the north face had made the summit.

The decision seemed to make sense, yet four days after I left, Scott McKee went back up and became the only climber to reach the summit that year, alone and in deteriorating weather. "You should have been there, Heidi," he said when he returned to Montana. "You would have made it."

For most of us, there is only the unattended
Moment, the moment in and out of time,
The distraction fit, lost in a shaft of sunlight,...
Or the waterfall, or music heard so deeply
That it is not heard at all, but you are the music
While the music lasts.

—T. S. ELIOT,

"The Dry Salvages"

THE LABYRINTH

I had somehow gotten off track in describing the summit bid on Kanchenjunga. Trying to hold on to that moment of deep comprehension, that sudden, elusive vision of the connection between all things, I felt an urgent need to circle back.

"So there was that *light* that I saw in the avalanche," I said, trying to verbalize my thoughts, "but there was also that vision of Kanchenjunga as a labyrinth, and the passages in the ice caves that the lama talked about."

"Kanchenjunga is where they're creating that Tri-National Peace Park, right?" Hiddle asked.

I was mildly surprised that a nonclimber was aware of the relatively recent efforts to establish a sanctuary in the Kanchenjunga Himal. "Yeah, it is. Why?"

"Been thinking about going there to photograph blue sheep. What was the trek like?"

It was on the trek to Kanch that I met the lama who told me about the labyrinth. Although I really wanted to focus on the connection between the light and the labyrinth, I didn't mind telling him the whole story.

SEVEN WEEKS BEFORE THE AVALANCHE, I WAS SITTING IN A hotel lobby in Kathmandu with Jon Pratt, the leader of the 1997 American-British expedition to Kanchenjunga. He had pieced together a team of climbers who hoped to climb a route on the northwest face in lightweight expedition style, without the use of bottled oxygen or high-altitude porters. My personal goal was to climb part, or all, of the route alone. Although I knew we would need to work together to fix ropes and establish high camps, my philosophy on 8,000-meter peaks is that it is best to think of the summit bid as a solo endeavor. No one can help you at those altitudes. The 120-mile approach was an important part of preparing for the climb, and to clear the cobwebs of civilization from my mind, I had decided to trek alone, despite the predictable objections from Jon and other members of the expedition.

"There are no villages above 3,400 meters," he warned me, "It's dangerous to trek alone up there. There's no one up there but Tibetan yak herders with big knives. A couple of Germans disappeared without a trace a couple of years ago. I mean, *I* wouldn't do it."

I couldn't help smiling. Jon was a veteran of many Himalayan expeditions, including a successful ascent of K2 and several epic solo journeys. He knew what it meant to accept risk and solitude. I thanked him and decided to go anyway.

The journey began at a tiny airfield in the terraced foothills near the village of Taplejung, where expeditions typically arrive with an entourage of Nepalis hired in Kathmandu: a guide, a cook, a liaison officer, and a *sirdar* to hire the porters. I had none of those, of course, and as I ferried my duffel bags back and forth to the edge of the grass landing strip, I felt conspicuously alone. Somehow, I needed to find two reliable porters without the assistance of a sirdar. My goal was to cover 120 miles and 14,000 vertical feet of rugged terrain in six days, each of us carrying 60-pound loads, without a cook or doctor or any of the other luxuries of organized trekking groups. I wanted porters who wouldn't balk if the weather turned bad, porters who would go beyond the village of Ghunsa, where expedition loads are usually transferred to yaks. And as a female, alone in one of the most remote regions in the Himalaya, I needed to find two men I could trust.

I was even more worried when I shuttled my loads to a local teahouse and my request for two *bhariyaa* (porters) to go to Base Camp in six days was met with puzzled looks of disbelief. Within minutes a small crowd had gathered around my bags outside the teahouse door. "No possible go Pangpema six days," muttered one old man. I folded my arms across my chest as I repeated the request—trying to look tougher—and eventually resorted to pulling out my down climbing suit and an axe with a freshly sharpened black pick from my duffel bag to prove my competence. I felt ridiculous, but the high-tech gear had the desired effect. The proprietor of the teahouse immediately sent someone out, and several cups of tea later I found myself weighing loads with the two Gurung porters who would be my companions for the next week: Chandra, a 21-year-old with the chiseled legs of an Olympic athlete, and Prem, a wiry, nimble 38-year-old father of five.

We spent the first night near a cluster of clay houses perched on the steep flank of a gorge carved by the Tamur River. Chandra called the place Linkim. It was not on any of my maps. I felt a flicker of doubt, wariness at being led off the established route, and then reminded myself that I was making a leap of faith and needed to establish a bond of instantaneous, unconditional trust. I shared my tent and food; Chandra and Prem shared their knowledge of the terrain—and their friends along the way.

I flopped down next to my pack to peel my boots off, rest, and stretch in the orange glow of the late afternoon sun. A woman was filling a jug from a spring that poured through a large rhododendron leaf wedged between two stones. Dozens of bats were darting through the air. Brush fires were burning across the gorge, glowing like feral eyes in the fading light.

It would be dark soon. I pulled a carabiner and sling from my gear, made a tripod for the stove, and began to brew water for our meal. Four or five children hovered near us, and as I squatted in the dirt, stirring peanut butter sauce into a foil package of freeze-dried Thai spicy chicken, I felt vaguely guilty about intruding in this still pristine little nook of Shangri-La. The metal in the stove, the plastic in my cup, the rubber in my soles—these are all exotic materials in such a world. Other materials like the high-tech microfleece in my jacket were entirely alien. And when I stopped to think about the materials I had left at home—the Teflon in the no-grease muffin pan, the silicon in the fax modem, the ethereal mass of electrons in the World Wide Web—I felt like an intruder, a creature from another planet.

For the next three days we followed the music of the Tamur and Ghunsa rivers, dancing across swaying suspension bridges and laboring up steep, twisted paths. At night we slept with the roar of the rapids and stars that crowded the sky like wildflowers in a field. The air was filled with lazy cloud shadows and the steady hum of bees. Like the petrified prayers on the *mani* stones and the venerable monks meditating up in remote caves, life in these valleys seemed to exist outside of time.

On the fourth day we reached Ghunsa, a small village of with wooden raised-platform houses and strings of prayer flags that fluttered in the wind. Here Prem and Chandra met old friends, and when we climbed the small wooden ladder and entered the smoky, dark womb of their house, we were greeted with smiles and *tomba*—a strong homemade barley beer served in a wooden gourd. I stretched my socks out to dry on a narrow plank bed and sat next to the fire, hugging my tired legs and allowing the restlessness that I usually feel at dusk to dissolve in the simple flow of the movements around me. The room was filled with the sounds of life: the feisty cry of a newborn, the tinkling of yak bells under the house, and the slow, steady grinding of a millstone.

The heavy stone was turned by the *hajar-amaa*, the grandmother of the house. I was mesmerized by the strength and grace of her movements. She noticed me staring, and suddenly laughed and invited me to help. I pulled on the handle. My movements were clumsy, and the stone immediately popped out of its well-worn groove. She laughed again, hammered it back in, and placed my hands closer to the stone, at the base of the handle. We rocked back and forth in a rhythmic, circular motion, her beautifully gnarled hand clasped firmly around mine.

The day after that I met the monks.

Chandra and I rose early, retraced our steps across the wooden bridge leading to Ghunsa, headed back toward Amjilasa, and then left the trail, winding up through the rhododendrons on a nearby hillside. As the undergrowth thinned, my heart was pounding wildly in my chest. It was spring, and the air was heavy with the coupling of male and female creatures, the smell of dung and birth. Although a mist still shrouded the slope, I could imagine the vivid green of the leaves, the ripples of sunlight and undulating thrusts of sprouting things that would fill the forest around me as soon as the sun crested the ridge above.

Near the top of the ridge we veered onto a path that wrapped around the contours of the land, dipping into ravines and arcing back under the shadows of cliffs. Each rocky promontory seemed to be a *lhap-so*, a worship site, marked with a *chorten* and sometimes a string of prayer flags.

I had not had time in Kathmandu to make an offering at the Boddhanath stupa, so Chandra was taking me to visit a lama, a Tibetan Buddhist monk, living in the hills to the west of Ghunsa. We would make an offering of a golden Power Bar and a khata, and ask for a *serkim*, a ritual in which the lama asks the deities for understanding and toleration of an activity. These ceremonies are used for any activity which might offend the gods—building a house, climbing a mountain, slaughtering a yak. Pangpema, the broad terrace that climbers use for a Base Camp on the northwest side of Kanchenjunga, is a sacred site, the footprint of the first lama to enter the region from Tibet, so it seemed particularly important to honor and respect the tradition.

As we wound our way along the path, a solitary griffon followed our movements, circling upward on an invisible thermal, soaring around a bluff, first leading, then following. We passed to the left of a wall of mani stones, most carved with the mantra of the bodhisattva of compassion, *om mani padme hom*, and then left the path again, climbing once more up a steep slope.

At the top, we paused to drink from the bottle of water in my pack. There was a moment of stillness, followed by a gusty wind that turned the leaves over and brought a new smell, the scent of juniper boughs burning. From somewhere above, I heard the distant, deep-throated sound of a monk chanting mantras, prayer-like invocations that develop mindfulness and awareness. The fullness of each sound hung in the air, hovering like a moth before it dissipated. Was it my imagination, or was the sound of the chanting answered by a higher, more distant sound from the opposite flank of the gorge behind us?

Scanning the hillside above while Chandra quenched his thirst, I finally spotted the *gompa*, situated at the base of a cliff.

It was a true gompa, more of a hermitage than a monastery, a cluster of stone structures on a precipice, exposed to the wind. I imagined the monks enduring the wind, snow, and rain as tests of strength and will hurled at them by hoary, ferocious demons. Demons, those menacing creatures that are forever tempting humans away from the path of awareness and devotion, are depicted in many of the Buddhist *thangkas*, the silk and cloth paintings that portray the deities and demigods. They seem to lurk in every corner, every cavern of the Buddhist cosmos.

We stopped at the entrance to the gompa, lungs rebelling against the thin air. A monk was seated outside in the lotus position, eyes half closed, spinning a small prayer wheel and still chanting, softly now. A second monk emerged from a small, dark room in a niche of the cliff, cradling a bundle of potatoes in the folds of his maroon robe. He acknowledged our presence and greeting—*Namaste*, we salute the spirit within you—with a slight nod and a smile, and then began to lay the potatoes out on a stone ledge under the window. *A vow of silence?* I wondered, recalling the black-robed Catholic monks I used to watch as a child, silently walking up and down the street in front of our house, unable to speak to women.

Chandra motioned for me to follow, and we entered a humble room, barely large enough to hold a bed, a small wooden table and bench. A narrow window next to the door directed a shaft of the gleaming white light of the mountains onto the opposite wall. In the corner of the room, on the flat wooden planks of the bed, a monk sat waiting. He smiled. I was surprised at the ascetic simplicity of his surroundings: no thangkas, no stone statues, no ancient Tibetan manuscripts. Just a bowl of water and a small cluster of yak butter lamps in an empty alcove next to the bed.

Chandra explained the purpose of our visit, and the lama nodded, rolled off the bed and slipped his feet into his sandals. He trotted out the door, smiling, a compact bundle of sinew and bronzed skin. When he came back, still smiling, he was carrying a small bowl of *tsampa*, barley flour, and a small branch of juniper.

Like other rituals, the *serkim* is not intended to bring good luck. Tibetan Buddhists believe that the gods will continue to either protect climbers or allow demons to lure them into harm's way regardless of whether or not a ceremony is performed. Instead of asking for benevolence, the ritual opens the faithful to achieve the levels of awareness that are needed to better recognize omens and opportunities. It is a deeply meditative discipline.

The lama sat in front of the alcove altar and began reciting mantras. The alcove, like the bare stone room, seemed to symbolize the womb of emptiness from which all things come. I watched him dip the tip of the juniper into the urn of water and flick it three times toward the altar. Water cannot be contained or possessed; like the spirit, it temporarily takes the shape of a container and then flows through the universe. He dipped his right hand into the tsampa and raised it in the air three times. On the third, he released the flour, tossing it toward the small flames of the lamps, and then brushed the remaining dust into my hair. I laughed: white hair for long life. We prostrated ourselves three times before the altar, in a demonstration of respect and abandonment of pride, and the lama produced a *sungdi*, a red string necklace with knots that are meant to protect climbers from harmful spirits that can lure them into a crevasse or into the path of falling things.

We presented our offerings in return and then stepped outside.

"A star with a tail is not good," the lama remarked, still smiling, gesturing toward the sky with a matter-of-fact sweep of his arm, "Maybe this is not the right time to try to climb Kanchenjunga."

I nodded. Yes, I had overheard a group of Sherpas in Kathmandu talking about the Hale-Bopp comet, which had appeared in the skies several weeks before. They too believed it was a bad omen. But going home simply because of a comet in the sky, after so many months of planning, was unthinkable. I had very real obligations to all of the sponsors, family, and friends who had supported me.

There are passages in the ice caves on Kanchenjunga, the lama continued to explain, places where the darkness gives birth to light, paths to Shambhala. Some places in the world, some spots on Earth, are mirrors of a larger reality, one that is too intense to perceive directly.

It is easy to get lost in the white paths, he said, and nodded towards the opposite side of the gorge. I looked. On the opposite flank of the gorge, still partially in shadow, a low-lying mist twisted in and out of the trees, creating patterns of dark and light, light and dark.

And suddenly I understood. It was a maze, a labyrinth, a twisted network of passages.

"MY SISTER AND I USED TO PLAY IN A LABYRINTH AS children," I told Hiddle idly, still thinking about the connection between a labyrinth and the light I saw in the avalanche on Kanchenjunga. "There was a field of cattails on our property, and one summer my father mapped out a maze and then rented a big industrial mower to carve the paths."

Places where the darkness gives birth to light. From darkness, light is born.

"The cattails must have been at least six feet high, and dense enough that you couldn't see through them. We would get completely lost."

There are spots in the world that are dangerous, mirrors of a reality that are too intense to perceive directly.

"The best part was sometimes he would put our rooster, Pick-adee, in at one end. Pickadee was the type of creature who could sense fear, and would come flying at your face with beak and scratching claws if he thought he could get away with it. With the twists and turns in the maze, we could outrun him, just barely. So we would creep around the corners, looking for him, screaming and running, playing with the fear and uncertainty."

Places that lure us to them with a magnetic kind of force.

Darkness—some call it danger or uncertainty or evil—is necessary for enlightenment, because it is only through confronting fear and anger that a higher energy, a truer state of being, is born. But are these spots with dangerous but sacred energy, like a clot in the flow of the universe, places where the normal laws of free will and cause and effect don't apply? Or are they like the knots in a tree trunk that mark branches, junctures, passages to another world?

Was there a beginning that day? I think there must have been one somewhere, lurking in the saffron folds of the monk's robes, in the ringing echoes of the chants, and the wraithlike patterns of the clouds hovering on the opposite flank of the gorge. But every time I revisit the scene in my mind, I can find nothing but monks and a visitor: cause and effect, action and reaction. Beginnings, as I have already said, are elusive, feline sorts of things.

WE NEEDED GAS. I PULLED OFF THE HIGHWAY AT A REST area called White River Junction, and stepped out of the car with my mouth and nose burrowed into the neck of my fleece jacket.

Hiddle met me at the pump.

"You know that climber I was telling you about, Wanda, the Polish climber who was the first woman to reach the summit of K2?" I asked, blowing on my hands while the gas flowed through the hose, "Or maybe I didn't mention her, I can't remember. She died on Kanchenjunga in 1992. I like to think she saw the labyrinth, too."

"Hold that thought. Just freeze frame it there for a while. I'm gonna go slay a dragon." He ambled off to smoke in the corner of the parking lot. As he walked, I could see him gazing at the snow falling from the black sky through long whistling puffs of smoke.

Twenty minutes later, we were back on the road.

"Tell me about Wanda," Hiddle said.

"She disappeared high on Kanchenjunga in 1992." I told him more about the legends of Kanchenjunga, the avalanches, the labyrinth. "My climb with Friedl Mutschlechner of Kanchenjunga's North Face was one of the most dangerous of my life," Reinhold Messner wrote after he had climbed the 14 highest peaks in the world. "It almost succeeded in extinguishing our spirit of life." The North Face of Kanchenjunga has challenged a whole parade of Himalayan luminaries: Messner and Mutschlechner; Bettembourg, Boardman, and Scott; Buhler, Habeler, and Zabaleta. All of these climbers struggled for their lives on the descent, with tents destroyed at 26,000 feet by the notorious winds of the Great Scree Terrace and high camps wiped out by the avalanches that pour down the face.

The North Face also claimed the life of the most prolific female climber in the history of Himalayan climbing, the Polish mountaineer Wanda Rutkiewicz, who disappeared after reaching 27,000 feet (8,300 meters) on May 12, 1992. She had succeeded on eight other 8,000-meter peaks, including Everest, K2, and Nanga Parbat. It was her third attempt to climb Kanchenjunga.

We will probably never know the full story of her last climb. Did she fall from the summit ridge, down the steep south face, or into a crevasse on the Yalung Glacier, thousands of feet below? Did she slowly freeze, waiting for the light of the morning? When her partner, Carlos Carsolio, met her on his descent from the summit, she was resting in a snow cave at 27,000 feet, determined to continue on her own. On all but a few nights each year, the cold winds raging over the summit pyramid would make such a decision fatal. Or did she reach the summit? It is tempting to think that she did and simply succumbed to exhaustion on the descent.

My own idea is plainly false and stubbornly misguided, but I cling to it because it terrifies me. I like to think that Wanda found the other exit to the labyrinth. Perhaps, as she was lying in her snow cave, and the cold and the dark and the ice engulfed her, she saw those streaks of light, the smooth, unambiguous flowing of the universe in a single direction. Perhaps she saw through the light into the darkness beyond.

"I lust after mountains," she said in a lecture in Vienna. "They attract me like magnets."

Wanda's mother, in an interview with one of her climbing partners, Gertrude Reinisch, commented, "Whenever Wanda was about to leave for an expedition, I used to go round her apartment and bless her. She was always in a great rush, surrounded by packing chaos. I never felt afraid for her; I had a feeling that nothing bad would happen to her, and she always promised not to take silly risks. But when she was leaving for Kanchenjunga, it was all so different. Her apartment was all neat and orderly. And Wanda nearly slipped away without my having drawn the sign of the cross on her forehead. I had to call out after her, and she seemed almost reluctant to come back. It was not the same. It was as though she were hiding something from me, as though she had plans. When her climbing companions came to tell me that she was dead, I said: 'No. I know that she's alive, but in a better place where she is happy.' She sometimes visits me in the night, and when she touches me I am lifted on a wave of strength and energy. She gives out silver rays which fill me with a great joy when they shine on me, and they hold me to life."

Gertrude left a plaque for Wanda at base of Kanchenjunga in 1995. It reads:

"Meine Furcht verschwand,
und ich verspürte
eine grosse Freiheit"
12 Mai 1992, Wanda Rutkiewicz

"My fear disappeared, and I experienced a great freedom."

The many men, so beautiful!
And they all dead did lie:
And a thousand thousand slimy things
Lived on; and so did I.

—SAMUEL TAYLOR COLERIDGE,
The Rime of the Ancient Mariner

THE YELLOW SLICKER STORY

Hiddle began to talk in a disconnected way about the effects of perestroika on the Polish and what he called fear of freedom. "Did climbers in Poland adjust easily to capitalist systems?" he queried.

I shrugged and didn't answer. Driving white-knuckled in the storm and squinting through the snow at signs plastered with ice and grime was getting to me.

"My grandfather had a story about people who grow used to struggling to survive," he said after a while.

"Your turn to tell, then. I'm beat. I need some real caffeine—the cup of coffee I grabbed back there was gnarly. Maybe we'll pull off at the next exit and try to find something open."

And so, as I battled the storm, Hiddle told a story about men at sea, about survivors who survived but couldn't live. I think he called it the story of the yellow slickers, but I'm not sure. I don't remember every detail perfectly. It went something like this:

ONCE THERE WAS A BOY WHO CAME FROM A LARGE FAMILY *who lived in a coastal village in southern France. It was a fishing village, and the boy spent many long hours on the wharf that stretched out like a long finger pointing to the waves and the vast open nothingness of the sea. Knowing nothing other than the sting of the salt on his tongue and the aching cries of gulls circling overhead, he longed to go out to sea when he grew up, to join the cadres of* marins *who returned every few months to hug their mothers and make mad and lusty love to their women behind barely drawn curtains.*

When the day finally came for the boy to leave, his cousins and his sisters and his mother and his new girlfriend, Marian, the one with a freckle on the inside of her thigh, came down to the wharf. His mother cried, his sisters kissed him, his cousins hugged him, and Marian gave him a yellow jacket. The village was poor, but families always saved up enough to give this one thing.

Two nights later, there was a thin crescent moon hanging in the sky. It was a grin—a yellow grin—beaming down though empty space and shattering into a thousand small grins on the waves of the black ocean below. The boy looked at it, at the star hanging next to the moon, and knew he should go back, should abandon the boat and its crew at the next port of call. It is common knowledge among sailors that something evil is about to happen whenever a star dogs the moon.

But when the ship came and went at the next port two days later, he came and went with it. The sea was the only way of life he had ever known.

And two days after that, the winds began to blow. By evening, it was a full gale.

The crew fought the storm day and night, night and day, for 20 days, some say 20 years. Bailing, hauling, desperately clinging on to the halyards, bracing themselves for a boarding wave, they moved from crisis to crisis. Repair the trysail, stow the hatch, relight a lantern, wedge themselves into a bunk in the fo'c'sle for a few fleeting moments of dreamless sleep. Struggling became an instinct, a reflex, a way of life. All this time, the rains poured endlessly into the sea, feeding the angry waves, and the waves tossed themselves up into the sky, refilling the clouds. The storm was around and on and in the boat, even inside the yellow jackets, in great sloshing waves of terror and adrenaline.

The yellow jackets were the things that, in a spinning, angry world of gray and black and frothing white, kept each man on board from being washed away in the storm. Yellow was the color of love, of safety, of hope and of home.

And then, after 20 days, the sea was calm.

Calm, or maybe even dead. The crew staggered around the deck, clutching at the bulkward and ropes because the sea was so calm that the ship rested firm and horizontal, like an oasis of land under their feet. They shielded their eyes from the foreign light of a forgotten sun and shouted to each other, as though they were still trying to shout over the roar of the wind and the waves. They held a huge celebration, brought the last bin of salted pork rinds up from the hold.

After the celebration a strange silence, a sort of sadness, descended on the ship. The wind that came with the storms was also gone, and there was nothing left to do but drift and wait for a new wind. The very thing they hoped for, freedom from the storms, became a burden, a thing to be feared, for now there was nothing but them, the ship, and the sea.

Even stranger than the silence were the yellow slickers.

Each man wore his slicker like a dream, a remnant of some yesteryear that he couldn't or didn't want to forget, a heavy shroud of fear and hope that weighed more than a murdered albatross. There were differences: some wore the jackets like sunshine; some wore them to hide from the sun; some wore them open, revealing further layers of yellow underneath; some wrapped them tight, realizing that underneath there was a new creature that none would recognize. Yes, underneath, there was a new creature. Underneath, every man's skin had turned yellow.

After two days of this strange calm, the boy—for he was still a boy, although he called himself a man—climbed up the rigging one night, all the way up to the gaff. He took off his yellow jacket, and discovered another underneath it, and another underneath that. He began to peel off the jackets one by one, like layers of an onion. Each layer released the collective memories of the crew—the crashing walls of waves, the foaming, spitting sea, the driving ice and sheets of lightning, the roar of wind and things smashing against the walls of the hull.

And then, when it seemed like there couldn't possibly be any more layers, when the fading blur of yellow high above the ship's deck had dwindled to just a pinprick of light, there was one final low growl of thunder, and rain. A cloud of yellow tears fell down through empty space, scattering into a thousand small tears on the black waves of the ocean below.

In the morning, there was a steady, warm westerly blowing. The ship's crew searched for the boy, but couldn't find him. Must have fallen overboard, they decided. Together they removed their jackets and set sail for home.

I WAS STUNNED. HIDDLE HAD TOLD THE STORY WITH SUCH unaffected intensity. He couldn't possibly have had any idea how apropos it was, how incredibly direct and simple the connection was with the Wanda that I had experienced. The storm, the controversy amongst the Polish climbers over her ascent of Annapurna in 1991— she was a receptacle for all their fears, all their uncertainties and unease in the presence of a new, unfamiliar calm. They very thing they had hoped for, freedom from the oppressive political system that made it difficult for them to acquire quality equipment and leave the country, had become a burden. Perestroika had left them with nothing to blame but themselves.

And then there were those yellow jackets.

The story carried me back to the vision I had had in the palm reader's place in Pindi, of Wanda peeling off one layer after another—and to yet another time and place, to an evening in August 1992, when I was standing in front of a kitchen sink in Massachusetts, hands soaked with soapy dishwater, staring silently at the image of a female climber in a yellow suit reflected in or through the black windowpane in front of me. It was one of those raw experiences, a few fleeting moments that contained the compressed emotions of an entire lifetime. I felt waves of emotion sweep through my body. Hope. Fear. Anger. Passion. Sorrow. And then it was gone.

At the center, after all the emotions were spent, there was nothing left.

A month or two later, I discovered a photo of the woman in my vision next to a little blurb in a climbing magazine. It was Wanda, of course.

Her life, I realized, was like the vapor that rises from a howling wolf's mouth on a cold blue morning. Unforgettable, but oh so evanescent, so malleable. Five months after she died, the world she knew had tweaked both her reality and her death to fit a comfortable, containable truth—she was exhausted and disenfranchised and lonely, they decided. Five years later, the signature of time was etched in the plaque left in her memory at the base of the mountain. Five decades later, her life will be only a dim memory for her remaining friends and family.

And five centuries later, only the mountain will be there, neither savage nor grand, just quiescent and mute, through all the changes in weather, light, and perception.

At this altitude the boundaries between life and death are fluid.

—PETER HABELER

FROZEN MINUTES

"Are you going to pull off?" Hiddle asked.

"Shout if you see something. Doesn't look like there's much around here."

We were on Highway 91, heading south. Our chances of finding a rest stop on this particular stretch of the road were about par with the chances of a snowflake on an iron griddle.

We were both slightly hunched over, squinting through the windshield and slipping and sliding at 35 miles per hour.

"So you never told me about what happened with your ex and that other guy," he said.

"On K2, you mean?" I asked.

"Yeah, I think that was it."

"What can I say?" For some reason I felt mildly irritated. "It was like living through a movie. All action and drama."

THE SCRIPT WOULD BEGIN, I SUPPOSE, ON JULY 4, 1998, the day after we reached Base Camp. Zee was playing card games with the Pakistani liaison officer (L.O.), Captain Jahanzeb, trying to educate him about American customs on our Independence Day.

"You don't have any fireworks?" He was pestering Jahanzeb in a boisterous, affected southern drawl. "How 'bout bombs instead? Can't we get one of those howitzers from the boys over at that mil'try base at Concordia? We could use 'em to trigger an avalanche. See that big snot of a glacier hanging over there? Can't you just imagine bringin' it down?"

Zee isn't exactly your average Texan dude rancher. Back in the U.S., he was an anti-American first-generation immigrant, a rebel on a quest for a cause. But as an American traveling in a foreign country, he switched roles and opinions, sometimes daily. Today he was pretending to be a guns 'n' bombs enthusiast.

Captain Jahanzeb was clearly enjoying the show. "Dynamite is better. You will need a helicopter. If we use your satellite phone to ring headquarters in Rawalpindi today," he pointed out, "we might get permission in, oh, maybe two years."

The captain's mission was to hang out for two months at 16,000 feet to ensure that we (1) weren't abducted by Indians or aliens, (2) didn't steal any of the Pakistani military secrets that are rumored to be stashed on the summit of K2, and (3) climbed the right mountain and the right route. Although L.O.s are required by Pakistani law to carry a gun for this post, attempting to enforce any law when the climbers are high on K2 would be unwise. So the standard recourse is to report infringements to the Ministry of Tourism in Islamabad at the end of the expedition. The Ministry is empowered to fine and ban violators. For climbers who are not planning to return to Pakistan, this is seldom a sufficient deterrent. For climbers who want to return in less than seven years, the rules are simple: (1) Don't do anything that might make the L.O. angry, and (2) Don't say anything that might make the L.O. angry. Which isn't to suggest that following the rules is necessarily simple.

We were lucky. Our appointed officer spoke English with the precision of a scholar, and he was endowed with a strong survival instinct. He was anxious to complete the mission with a minimum of bureaucratic hassle so that he could get married two months later and begin to procreate.

Discovering that explosives were restricted to the active frontiers about ten miles away, Zee decided gambling would be the next best thing, and he spent the rest of the afternoon instructing Captain Jahanzeb on the finer points of blackjack.

"What happens," Jahanzeb asked, "if I deal from the bottom of the deck?"

"I'll report you," Zee growled, "to the Ministry of Card Games."

We spent the rest of the day lounging around Base Camp, piling up rocks to make tent platforms, heating icy water for laundry, coiling ropes, hooking up the solar panels and other electronic paraphernalia. The process of establishing a home in the middle of a frozen nowhere is a strange business. One minute you are grunting as you heft a large rock for a table or scratching your head about where to find water, and the next minute you are flipping up the silver cover of your laptop and beaming signals to a distant artificial star.

Satellite telephones have become a standard piece of equipment for Himalayan expeditions, but in 1998 they were still as rare as yeti tracks. They were also the subject of many heated barroom debates prior to our expedition. Phones are an ethical necessity, one of my climber friends propounded. They reduce anxiety in the lives of your loved ones. No, lights and telephones are evil, another climber friend argued. They disrupt natural rhythms. They disturb your sleep and thought processes. "Phones," yet another climber friend said, "are for people who can't stand their own company."

It might be useful to note that the first climber friend has children. The second two don't.

Our decision to bring the satellite phone was tempered by two provisos. One, we would power everything via solar juice. All three of us absolutely refused to bring generators into the wild. Among other problems, they're so noisy that you can't hear an avalanche pouring off the mountain or a glacier creaking under your tent. Two, we would figure out how to use the phone before we transported it halfway around the world.

A satellite phone, I discovered in the process of learning how to use it, is a PAPOT (Pretty Awesome Piece of Technology). And, as with any PAPOT, there's a whole bunch of jargon associated with it. When I went to a company called CSSI for training on the unit, I learned that our phone was an MES. It was an MES that communicated with an LES via an NCS. The link between the MES and the LES was a bird that you find by calculating elevation and azimuth. There are four Inmarsat birds: the AORW, the AORE, the IOR, and the POR. K2 is in the spot beam coverage of the IOR.

K2, with its sheer black faces and gracefully fluted slopes of snow, has a magnetic allure for many climbers. At 28,250 feet (8,611 meters), it juts into the troposphere and disrupts the flow of atmospheric currents, producing eddies of bad weather.

Riding a Pakistani junga bus on the
Karakoram Highway—an engineering
feat that winds through the debris of
a geological collision zone formed by the
world's four highest mountain ranges—
is not for travelers with weak hearts.

The daughters of our Pakistani host, Salman Ali, can now attend one of the new schools established by the Central Asia Institute in the vicinity of K2.

Members of the K2 98 team contemplate the challenge of sizing 72 Pakistani porters for shoes donated through the SupPorters Project. Although expeditions are required to provide basic equipment, the items available in Pakistan are inadequate for the harsh conditions and challenges of the trek.

My first glimpse of K2
was from the summit
of GII, another of
the world's fourteen
8,000-meter peaks.

Unlike most other high camps, Camp 4
on GII is not scoured by high winds or
avalanches. It is a high-altitude museum,
a field of rime-covered tent skeletons—mute
testimony to the powerful human urge
to survive.

Dehydrated and dazed after the avalanche,
I decided to continue up to the next camp.
Climbing—like survival—seemed an instinct
to me, a reflex.

I was mesmerized
by the silence and the
shimmering waves
of heat floating above
the snow. Another
avalanche had swept
the couloir clean and
there was no trace
of my struggle from
the day before—
just a smooth arc up
to a lip of ice
500 feet above.

On the north side of K2 in 2000, I realized after another small avalanche at Camp 3 that the concept of killer waves of snow had somehow become part of a day's work. It is easy to let the threshold of acceptable risks rise.

Of course, if you're a jargon phobe, the folks at CSSI explained, there's always the easy way of operating the phone. You flip the antenna up, move around until the beeping gets fast, and then dial 00 plus your number.

Receiving calls is even easier. The phone rings. You pick it up.

In the end, it doesn't matter whether beaming messages to loved ones from the mountain is an evil ethical necessity or a means of escaping one's inner voices. Satellite phones continue to evolve. All that matters is they're easy to use.

"Ease," you see, is not a word that applies to most other Base Camp activities, even on rest days. Lounging at 16,000 feet is simply not equivalent to sipping frosty drinks on a Caribbean cruise. Most of the time that climbers would prefer to spend in blissful contemplation of a mountain is spent in alleviating some new discomfort. The wind blows, and you are cold. The sun hits your tent, and you start sweating in your sleeping bag. It starts to snow, and you have to pull your boots on and climb over the glacial moraine to relieve your bowels. Your fingers are cracked from the cold and lack of oxygen, and you have to apply an antiseptic grease. Little capillaries in your lungs swell and ooze fluid into the alveoli, and you have to cough to breathe.

Climbers typically spend a day or two after they arrive at Base Camp acclimatizing before they make the first foray up to a higher elevation on the mountain. Even at 16,000 feet your body is reeling from the decrease in pressure and oxygen. Helicopter pilots who fly at this altitude must wear oxygen masks, and even experienced climbers, if they are not careful in regulating fluid intake, can succumb to nausea, headaches, and other symptoms of altitude sickness.

A physician friend once told me it would be a good idea to wait at Base Camp until your kidneys start pumping out a hormone that will trigger the mass production of red blood cells in the marrow of your bones.

How long does that take? I wanted to know.

Oh, probably three or four weeks, he answered.

Two days after we arrived at Base Camp, Chris, Zee and I began climbing up to Camp 1. To get to the Abruzzi Ridge, where the camp is situated, climbers must first climb through the Godwin-Austen icefall, an intricate mess of ice pinnacles, rushing glacial rivers, delicate ice bridges, and crevasses. Finding a path through it is like trying to find your way through a human-size labyrinth. Except the walls are ice, not hedges, and every now and then those building-sized pinnacles fall down.

Route finding is one of the finer points of Himalayan climbing. When you look at a photo or stare up at the looming hulk of the mountain from Base Camp, it seems easy. You just follow that ridge-line here, up to that couloir, and then on to that beautifully sculpted arête there. Climbing the mountain, though, is another story. The thing that looked like a yellow blob through the telescope turns out to be a 500-foot-wide band of rock with vertical smears of ice. There is a single passage through it, a 50-foot-high cleft that you call House's Chimney. That thing you called the "little triangle of rock" at Base Camp? As you try to climb it, it morphs into the Black Pyramid, an ominous 1,000-foot section of vertical rock and ice.

The footprints of the Italian team sharing our route had been erased by a snow squall the night before, so instead of leaving at the customary 2:00 a.m., when the snow is firm, we had decided to wait until daybreak. After trudging through knee-deep soft snow and sludgy ice an hour out of Base Camp, I weighed the disadvantages of climbing at night against the problems of climbing after the sun has hit the glacier. Would trying to establish a route via headlamp have been better? I wasn't sure. Then I broke through a slushy snow bridge into a thigh-deep pool of blue ice water, and knew the answer.

As Chris watched me flounder at the end of the rope, hunting for firm ground, he said, "you have probably just set a high-altitude swimming record."

We continued climbing for another five hours, stashed a pile of ropes an hour below Camp 1, and then returned to Base Camp to rest and load up our packs with gear for the next trip.

TWO DAYS LATER, WE REACHED CAMP 1, ONLY TO BE FACED with the unwelcome prospect of climbing back down and then back up a thousand feet to retrieve the remainder of the ropes.

Gravity is a fickle lover. When you're going down, following the natural path of things that fall, it caresses you, encourages you, carries you. You clumsily plunge-step down a powdered snow slope, delicately front-point down a couloir of ice, dance from stone to wobbly stone on a scree slope, and gravity is always present, urging you to continue. As soon as you move in any other direction, however, things are quite different. Up, for example. Gravity does not like up.

Going down to retrieve the gear at the cache site would be easy, a quick spider descent down ten lengths of fixed rope. Going up, we knew, would take triple the time, and ten times the energy. Zee volunteered to stay at Camp 1 and improve the tent platforms. Chris and I agreed to go down.

We were anxious to get back up to the warm sleeping bags in the tents, so as soon as we reached the cache, we slung our packs down and hastily began to divvy up the load.

Whumph! Our hearts skipped a beat, and we stood rigid for several seconds. While we were busy loading our packs, a rock bowling ball had broken loose from the cliffs above and careened past the cache, skipping down the steep slope and leaving fresh snow craters on impact. The nearest crater was only two feet from Chris's left leg.

We stared at each other for a few wide-eyed moments.

"It's O.K. It didn't hit us," Chris reasoned.

Don't argue with an optimist, I told myself. And so we finished packing our loads and headed back up the slope. The steps that we had so carefully kicked the day before, though, had been obliterated by a group of six climbers from the Italian team that had returned to Base Camp the night before, and so climbing the slope was once again an arduous task. Chris's size-12 feet would have left nice cruise-ship-size platforms for me to step into, but his legs are proportionally long, and I would have been hyperventilating trying to match his steep steps. So I very generously offered to lead.

To pass the time, we decided to play the Game of Falling Things. This is a little like the "find the letter Q" game you play with kids on a long drive in the car. Only instead of looking for letters, you look for fusillades of granite.

Our route up to Camp 1 followed a cracked spine of rock and ice, with a vast snow slope on the right and a jumbled mess of twisted rock bands on the left. The entire snow slope belonged to Chris. The twisted rock bands were mine. One falling object was worth one point.

Chris was already way ahead, 1-0, because the missile that had almost hit us had pogoed across the snow slope. Then my foot knocked a rock loose. It bounced down the rock spine a few times and then hit a right-angled rock that jettisoned it down the snow slope.

"Two to nothing," Chris said.

"That's my rock," I retorted, "I knocked it loose."

I noticed the familiar dull, oxygenless ache in my calves. It took me four breaths to get two sentences out.

Twenty minutes later, Chris said, "So I get the point because you shouldn't have knocked a rock loose."

Twenty minutes after that, I said, "No, it's my point. There's no one below us, so it's a good time to clear loose stuff."

The liners of my boots were pressing deep into my shins, and to balance the shin pain against the calf pain I was taking very precise, controlled steps, counting steps, counting breaths, counting steps again.

An hour later, we crested the final snow ridge to Camp 1.

"I still get the point because it went down my side. And you should get a point deducted for knocking it off," Chris said as he clipped his ascender into the final section of rope. "Three to zero."

I knocked the snow off my crampons and leaned against a rock, smiling and shaking my head. You can't argue with a stubborn optimist, I reminded myself. At least we didn't get taken out by any of the game pieces.

Inside the tent, I found Zee melting a pot of snow. He had spent the previous two hours digging deeper holes for the snow-pocket stakes we used to anchor the tents, and he was clearly in a foul mood.

"This tastes like a mixture of soggy cardboard and Elmer's glue," he greeted me with a frown. He was trying to down an entrée of plain oatmeal, and the contents of the cup were not agreeing with his palate. "And don't tell me it's the altitude," he added as I opened my mouth to respond, "Cardboard doesn't taste good at sea level, either."

"You want me to add something to it?" I asked. "We've got mustard. Or hot chocolate. Or Power Gel."

After several minutes of grumbling and muttering choice words as he rummaged through the little sack of food in the corner of the tent, he opted for the strawberry-banana Power Gel, which he consumed without the oatmeal. "It wouldn't have done anything for the texture," he explained when I gave him a reproachful look.

Eating at altitude is not easy. For one, you have to melt snow to cook anything, and to melt the snow, you have to get it first. Climbers usually fill an empty tent bag with chunks of icy snow when they arrive at a high camp. To get the snow out of the bag into the pot, you have two options: (1) gingerly pick the chunks out with your bare hands; or (2) scoop the chunks out with gloves. The first results in cold fingers. The second results in water with a slight glove-fuzz flavor. I prefer glove fuzz to cold fingers, but not every climber agrees with me on this very delicate subject.

Things like glove fuzz and sheer exhaustion and carbon monoxide poisoning from cooking inside a tent are not the main obstacles to eating, though. The real challenge is that the higher you go, the more your appetite diminishes. Food, especially food with a high fat content, requires two ingredients for digestion: oxygen and water. These two particular items are not in abundant supply on K2. So the body responds by decreasing the demands for food intake, progressing as the severity of the oxygen deprivation increases from lack of appetite to nausea and then to vomiting.

This description is, of course, a gross oversimplification of merely one aspect of the physiological response to altitude. A climber cannot go directly to 16,000 feet (Base Camp) without prior acclimatization. If he did, he would die, most likely of pulmonary or cerebral edema. There simply isn't enough oxygen in the air. At altitudes above 22,000 feet (Camp 2), it is impossible to survive indefinitely. For this reason, extreme altitudes are sometimes called the death zone (by media and the nonclimbing public, not by climbers themselves).

So how do climbers reach heights of up to 29,000 feet without supplementary oxygen? The age-old, time-tested process is to climb high and sleep low. By climbing to incrementally higher altitudes over a period of four to ten weeks, you trigger the responses in the body that enable it to adapt. In response to hypoxia and reduced atmospheric pressure, little alarms go off in your renal glands, which send a hormone called erythropoietin to the bone marrow. The marrow factories go into overdrive. Your red blood cell count shoots up, increasing your blood's ability to carry oxygen. There is a subtle (and not well understood) shift in the pH of your blood, which increases the oxygen affinity (the "stickiness," my physician friend calls this) of your hemoglobin. And by sleeping low after you have exposed yourself to an increased level of hypoxia, you grant your body the respite that it needs to make all these small miracles occur.

As Zee dumped his oatmeal outside the door of the tent, I watched every movement of his face, his eyes, his hands, wondering whether his lack of appetite was due to the altitude or his foul mood. The aches and emotional scars of the previous years had started to heal in the process of working together to plan and execute the expedition, but I was still wary, waiting to see how our bodies and emotions adjusted to the rigors of being at altitude. Strange things sometimes happen to climbers' emotions on the mountain, even under the best of circumstances, possibly because the process of generating red blood cells is so hormonal.

Something happened in that brief interval, somewhere in between the moment that Zee's hand unzipped the tent door and the point at which the falling coagulated mass of oatmeal hit the snow. Time froze for a few moments, or minutes, or years, circling back in on itself, spiraling down into the depths of my memory.

Our marriage, I realized in those few frozen minutes on K2, was like the mass of oatmeal lying in the snow. It was clotted, coagulated, a relationship in which our emotions were no longer fluid, a relationship in which we could no longer openly trust and share.

At that moment, I suddenly knew that we wouldn't live happily ever after. I had tried, but we had come to the end of our path together. Zee had taught me the art of expanding the soul through climbing; I had taught him the discipline of enriching the mind through education. He had tried to show me how to overcome fear; I had done everything I could to guide him through anger.

We need to climb together again, he had argued before the expedition. We need time to revisit those roots of our love.

But even the roots were frozen.

TWO WEEKS LATER, WE CLIMBED TO CAMP 1 FOR A FOURTH time, still trying to push our way up to Camp 2. The high-pressure system that surged in like a wave from the north at the beginning of July had receded, leaving an atmosphere instability that wreaked havoc with our plans. The day before, we had left the front doors of our single-wall tents unzipped while we cooked, leaning out into the snow on our elbows to suck in deep drafts of the crisp air and soak up the views of Chogolisa and Broad Peak. Now the doors were unzipped only a crack, just enough to poke our noses out to collect snow for melting. A meter of fresh snow had been dumped outside our tent during the night, and the wind had been pounding on the walls in fitful, insistent gusts.

Every forecasting service we had contacted prior to coming to K2 pinpointed the region as a "transition area," an area of unusually unstable, unpredictable weather. "From satellite photographs, it looks like the mountain is such a prominent feature," one meteorologist told me, "that it creates its own weather."

When a high-pressure front moves in from the north, from China, it pushes the "transition zone" south toward the Bay of Bengal. The good-weather window is typically signaled by strong north winds. When the high-pressure front retreats, you can see the bank of clouds from the south pour over Chogolisa like a wave. Or at least this is the local lore.

There had been no sign of a front moving in behind Chogolisa the night before, and our altimeters had been stable, so when dawn brought gray skies and the roar of gale-force winds high on the mountain, we decided to weather the storm. We had carried five days of food up for three days of working, hauling loads and fixing ropes. We were prepared to wait for at least a couple of days.

The decision was a hard one, complicated by the fact that two of the other three teams had decided to return to Base Camp. Sleeping at altitude helps with the acclimatization process, but it also rapidly depletes your reserves of mental and physical energy. Camp 1, at 19,850 feet (6,050 meters), is just shy of the summit of Denali, the highest point in North America.

The other team remaining on the mountain, a trio of Turkish climbers, decided to spend the day trying to catch a gorak, one of the large black birds circling over the camp, to supplement their dwindling food supply. Around dinner time, when they still hadn't managed to catch anything, one of them came over to our tents to demonstrate their most recent innovative solution, a device they called the Crampon Trap.

"You put the crampons like this," he explained, grinning, holding them with the points apart at one end like a huge, menacing jaw of teeth, "with a stone at the end to open them, and a string attached to the stone. You put a little bit of food in the middle, and when the bird comes, you pull the string, and *snap!* Dinner."

In our hypoxic state, we agreed that the plan had some merit, and offered a can of tuna for the bait.

THE FOLLOWING MORNING, WE DISCOVERED THAT OUR patience had been rewarded. The air had a new smell when we woke, and when we uncurled our stiff bodies enough to unzip the tent door, our eyes confirmed what our minds already knew. The storm was beginning to evaporate.

A cold golden sun was barely visible through the swirling, cotton-thick mist, and the wind had abated. But the deep fresh snow on the ledge where our tents were perched gave me pause: Did we need to wait for the snow to consolidate? Would the route be avalanche-prone? No, I reasoned, most of the route above was on rock. It was time to move up to Camp 2.

Climbing to Camp 2 on the Abruzzi Ridge is an intricate dance on a long, steep slope of mixed rock and ice. Without acclimatization, it would take us about six hours to gain 2,000 feet of altitude, and we wanted to return to Camp 1 for the night. We needed to move soon. I had no desire to be caught out late in unstable weather above 20,000 feet, to become a Popsicle on a rope. With only one stove between the three of us, melting snow to fill our bottles took an agonizing 90 minutes. Finally, at 9:30 a.m., we were ready to go.

As we climbed, the heavy mist made everything seem distant. My body felt surprisingly strong and agile, but nothing seemed to be moving around me. I balanced on a tenuous hold, crampons scratching across a smooth granite surface. Hadn't I touched this rock before? I ran my mitt across it. It was an old stone with a message that could no longer be deciphered. There was something eerily familiar about the sequence of movements, the smell of the crisp snow, the rock promontories in this harsh, distant corner of the world.

A shout from Zee caused me to swing around, and my breath caught. Several thousand feet above us, the north summit of Broad Peak had just sliced a window in the clouds. It was a sight worth shouting about. And then it was gone. The cloud curtain closed. We continued climbing.

An hour later, Zee shouted up again. "I'm going down. My feet are cold," I heard him say. The effects of altitude, cold, and concentration had slowed my mental processes, and my mind struggled to respond to what he was saying. We were about halfway to Camp 2. Should we all go down, or should I let him descend alone? At that point in the expedition, there was an umbilical cord of fixed ropes running to Camp 1, so the descent was reasonably safe for a single climber.

Chris and I were carrying two tents, a stove, food, a shovel, fuel, 500 feet of rope—everything we needed for real estate development at Camp 2. Our hands and feet were warm. Zee had another 500 feet of rope, but we could stash that on the fixed lines and then pick it up later. No, I reasoned, if Chris and I descended, it would wreak havoc with our plans. Best to continue.

I tried to shout some words of encouragement to Zee, to remind him that his warmer high-altitude boots were down at Base Camp, but only a nonsensical string of disconnected phrases came from my weak lungs and foggy brain. Before I could think of something coherent, he had tied off his pack and was rappelling down to Camp 1.

As I watched him begin the descent, I was apprehensive. We had already argued about the details of the route, the fixed lines, and the logistics of establishing camps. What would his reaction be to my decision to continue upward?

A few hours later, Chris and I were facing a vertical band of yellow rock, the final fortress on the route to Camp 2. We had made excellent time, but the wind was driving snow. As I started up the wide crack called House's Chimney that leads to the gentler snow slopes above, I realized that my hands were cramped and numb inside my mitts from gripping the cold metal shafts of my axes.

I tried to use the solid holds on the left side of the chimney, but my hands were wooden. My axes were equally useless on the thin runnel of ice that lined the cracks and angles. No matter how gently I swung the pick, the ice shattered in place after possible place, revealing only smooth rock. Finally I resorted to using the pick of the axe to hook the handholds. My crampons skittered and slipped on the rock as I inched up, but with intense focus and carefully balanced axe placements, I felt relatively secure.

Half an hour later, Chris and I were standing on Camp 2. It is a high-altitude junkyard, a field of rime-covered tent skeletons, with the remains of high-altitude struggles for survival buried in the snow. We spotted a brand-new Grivel axe and several canisters of fuel, but we had no desire to retrieve them. It somehow seemed like bad karma to try to profit from others' losses.

Death... It's the only thing we haven't succeeded in completely vulgarizing.

— ALDOUS HUXLEY

REQUIEM

"Wa-hoo!" I could hear Zee shouting below. We were descending to Base Camp at record speed, glissading on our rear ends down a steep slope on the north side of the Abruzzi Spur. With the picks of our ice axes digging into the snow to (more or less) control the rate of descent, we had discovered that it was the fastest nonfatal way to get off the mountain. Probably not the wisest thing to do after a deep, fresh snowfall. But the idea of a thousand-foot sled ride and french fries for lunch at Base Camp was tempting enough to override any vestiges of Darwinian sagacity, and so we were whooping and hollering our way down the hill.

Two of the Turkish climbers, Ugur and Sehran, had been slowly rappelling down the fixed ropes behind us, but monkey see, monkey do. After a few minutes of deliberation, they, too, were rushing down K2 on their rear ends. "Thanks for giving us this very good idea," Ugur grinned at the bottom. We were all slightly giddy with the fun and foolishness of what we had just done. My brain was awash with enough adrenaline that I wanted to spend two hours climbing back up just to do it again, but my stomach very quickly vetoed this idea.

The five of us—Zee, Chris, myself, Ugur, and Sehran, were the last climbers to retreat from the mountain after days of frustrating, unpredictable, unstable weather. We had hoped to continue, maybe even finish, fixing the lines to Camp 3, but the weather gods had other plans. A nervous south wind had been blowing for over a week, and storm after storm had pummeled the mountain, dumping a heavy blanket of snow on the upper flanks.

To vent the frustration, Chris, Zee, and I were focusing on the task of shooting footage for a National Geographic TV documentary. We were taking still shots to supplement the footage as we descended through the icefall, and in our restless, happy-go-lucky state of mind, the cues and responses rapidly degenerated from the mildly annoying to the ridiculous.

"Hold that death-defying position!" I shouted to Chris. He was perched at the top of a serac, a 20-foot ice marshmallow, looking dubiously at the footholds on the descent side. "Wait, no, can you come down about two feet? Great. Now, can you pick your left foot up, look directly up at the sky so there are no shadows on your face, and, umm, do something interesting with your ice axe? I got it! How about a fall? A dramatic photo op would be good."

Chris obliged, miming an exaggerated tumble down the serac, landing in a snowy heap at my feet. "Did you get it?" he asked.

"Umm, well, I got a great shot of the landing, but I didn't have the right shutter speed for that action-packed descent. Could you do it again?"

He laughed and stepped across the stream behind me. As I followed him, it was my turn to look dubious. The same easy stride across the stream for Chris was a long-jump record for me. And the consequences of not making it—soggy boots—were chilling.

"I'm going to set the camera to the rapid-sports-action mode," Chris called. "How about a splash? You know, a dramatic photo op."

As he pulled the camera out of its pouch, my legs were suddenly seized with a surge of adrenaline. I sailed through the air with the energy of a Hollywood superhero, clearing the stream in a single bound and landing with the grace of a deer on the opposite side. Well, OK, maybe the landing wasn't very graceful. And the jump was five feet, not fifty. But at least I made it.

"Not fair," I growled as I caught up to Chris. "You ought to be given a handicap for long legs."

He instantly dropped to his knees and began shuffling along beside me.

A little while later we were faced with another Terrifying Stream Crossing. I turned around to see if Chris would attempt it on his knees. Instead, he was lying on his back in the snow on the far side, camera pointed up in the air.

"What are you doing?" I yelled.

"Taking a picture of K2 upside-down," he shouted back. I looked up at the mountain. The top half was covered by a swirling mass of clouds. Oh well. I shrugged and grinned.

Someday Chris will be sitting in an office, surrounded by catalogs and photo slides, and a very important photo editor from a magazine with a huge circulation will call and say, "You wouldn't happen to have a stormy, upside-down image of K2, would you?" And Chris will say, "Yeah, sure" with a blasé nonchalance that suggests that all good climbers have taken *that* shot.

BELOW THE ICEFALL IS A LONG STRETCH OF RELATIVELY FLAT glacier where the debris from avalanches rolling off the shoulder of K2 fans out in a two-mile-wide crescent. The avalanches, pouring down a funnel that starts at about 23,000 feet (7,000 meters), can siphon huge quantities of snow off the shoulder. One of the avalanches we had watched from Camp 1 rolled all the way across the glacier and up the north flank of Broad Peak, leaving a pile of snow and ice 30 feet deep.

Snow and ice aren't the only things that come down. On the way back to Base Camp, the three of us stumbled across the body of a climber, lying face down, partially naked, in the rubble of the glacier. A tangled mess of clothing lay in a pool of ice water several feet away, with a dark hand protruding from a bright turquoise and fuchsia sleeve. There were wisps of wavy hair around the half-smashed skull with half a mouthful of teeth and one eye socket. There was a carabiner clipped to a loop of rope around the neck.

Every detail of the shattered corpse told a story of suffering. I wanted to cradle the body in my arms, to comfort it, to coax the anguish out of its broken face. Of course I couldn't. The bottom half of the torso was encased in ice. The sun had thawed parts of the body, and noxious liquids were a problem. So we simply marked the spot and returned later with gloves, bags, and a litter to carry the remains to Base Camp.

The body, we realized when we returned, was definitely male, with European clothing and European-style dental fillings. Bits of clothing were spread in a 50-foot radius around the body, and one of the shirts was silk-screened with the name Maurice. After looking at photos in books at Base Camp, we were reasonably certain that the body belonged to a French climber named Maurice Barrard.

Maurice and his wife, Liliane, had reached the summit of K2 together on June 23, 1986. They were climbing with their teammate Wanda Rutkiewicz, and another French climber, Michel Parmentier. Wanda and Liliane were the first two of the five women who have climbed K2.

In her biography of Wanda, *Caravan of Dreams*, Gertrude Reinisch provides a beautiful description of Wanda, Maurice, and Liliane's experience on the summit:

Wanda wrote the date and time, her own name and that of Liliane Barrard on a piece of card, over the proud legend "First Women's ascent," wrapped the card in a little plastic bag and secured it under a stone just to the north of the main summit. As the time passed, Wanda began to feel uneasy. Finally she could wait no longer and started down to meet the others. When at last they appeared she climbed back to the summit with them. Bursting with pride, Maurice said "We're the highest couple in the world," and hugged Liliane, who was weeping with joy, and said, "It's the first time I've ever been on a summit in such perfect weather. I can see the whole world." Then she exclaimed, "But what's this? The other mountains are growing higher. We're not the highest anymore, Wanda. Why not?" Wanda was experiencing the same optical illusion, and she could no more explain it than Liliane. "It was extraordinary and deeply impressive—as though we had become the innermost centre of the Universe. It must have been wonderful to share a moment like that with a partner. I felt a little envious and rather sad."

ON THE DESCENT FROM THE SUMMIT, DARKNESS OVERTOOK the group, and they were forced to spend a cold night at 27,200 feet, where they had bivouacked the night before. Crammed into a two-person tent without sleeping bags, they huddled together, tried to warm fingers and toes, slipped in and out of consciousness, fighting the devastating effects of altitude. Dawn brought a surge of energy, and Michel and Wanda, moving faster than the Barrards, moved down through swirling clouds to Camp 3, at 24,300 feet. Wanda, with frostbitten fingers and a blackened nose, decided to continue down to Camp 2, while Michel paused to melt snow and wait for the Barrards. The heavy skies obscured his view of the route. Wanda had last seen them just below their bivouac site, in the vicinity of the Bottleneck, a steep, narrow chute between seracs and a band of cliffs.

Michel melted snow and waited for two days. The Barrards never arrived. On the morning of the 25th, he awoke to high winds and heavy snow. Wanda's tracks from two days before had been erased, and as he staggered around the exposed plateau of the shoulder looking for the beginning of the fixed ropes, climbers at Base Camp tried to guide him by radio according to his descriptions of the features in the snow and their memories. He eventually stumbled on a urine-stained mound of ice near the top of the ropes, and was able to make it back down to Base Camp safely.

Liliane's twisted body was found several days later on the God-win-Austen Glacier, at the foot of the southeast face. Wanda and several of the other climbers on the mountain that year buried her at the Gilkey Memorial above Base Camp. Maurice's body was not recovered at the time. Whether they were swept down the 10,000-foot southeast face by a small avalanche, or simply stumbled and fell out of exhaustion, we will never know.

The loss of life is difficult, and no one will ever be able to persuade me that death is or should be an easy or painless process. No form of separation is easy. When I gave birth to a child, I wanted to feel all of the natural pain and the numb relief and ecstasy that follows it. When I die, I want the same. Dying is a process as important as the process of birth. It is important to reflect about it, to talk about it, to consciously embrace the process as an important step on a journey.

But what, I wondered, of the obviously violent mode of death Maurice and Liliane had experienced? Did they have time for reflection at the end? Time is a river, a nonlinear flow of interrelated objects in space. When objects are caught in a powerful eddy, minutes can seem to last forever. Perhaps, as Maurice and Liliane entered that realm of falling things, spinning through two miles of space to the glacier below, time became a whorling funnel, a vortex that stretched seconds into minutes, years, maybe even an eternity.

UNABLE TO CONTACT MAURICE'S DAUGHTER VIA SATELLITE phone or e-mail, we decided to bury his body with Liliane's. Several months later, with the help of the French embassy in Islamabad, National Geographic TV producers were able to contact Maurice's daughter, Claire Barrard. Ms. Barrard confirmed that the choice of the Gilkey as a burial site was appropriate.

The journey up to the Gilkey Memorial, carrying the body of one dead climber and a plaque for another, wasn't easy. A bitter, strong south wind was blowing, with gusts of sleet and snow. The memorial is an odd testimony to the savage indifference of the mountains, a five-foot-high memorial cairn perched on a ledge 100 feet above Base Camp. It is covered with plaques and prayers for climbers who have lost their lives on K2 and Broad Peak. Underneath, in a shallow tunnel, are the remains of others.

The plaque we carried was for an American climber named Rob Slater, sent by his parents. Rob and his partner, Alison Hargreaves, reached the summit of K2 on August 13, 1995, but disappeared during the descent when they were overtaken by a high-altitude storm. Rob had spent much of the season waiting for the elusive north wind to blow, frustrated by the unusually bad weather. Like us, they had been trying to climb in an El Niño year. We tied his plaque to another one left for Alison.

"Well, we didn't know Maurice," Zee mused as we finished the process of burying his body, "but we know what drew him here."

The plaques and plates at the Gilkey were all written in memory of competent, skilled climbers, and it is almost impossible not to return with serious questions about your motivation to climb. As I looked at the climbers around me—Zee, Chris, and others who had joined us—the line between life and death seemed impossibly thin. I saw each one of us in turn, walking, vanishing. The risk, the danger, seemed to have a new presence. It walked with us.

RISK AND DANGER ARE IMPORTANT PARTS OF HIGH-ALTITUDE climbing. Most climbers will admit that danger does play some role—maybe even that they actually enjoy the peculiar, delicious, chalky taste of fear—although they'll temper the admission with a disclaimer such as "But that's not why I climb."

Admitting that we are riskmongers or adrenaline junkies is not fashionable, especially after the recent hullabaloo about the 1996 Everest tragedy. Still, there is something essential about the possibility of real loss, even death, and without the presence of danger many climbers would quit. Honing your ice-climbing skills on a two-story ice cube simply isn't the same as climbing, creeping, up a delicate, unstable icefall, where many two-story ice cubes can topple on you at any time. The first of these two activities leaves you with the pride of self-discipline and the warm glow of accomplishment. The second leaves you with that hair-raising, skin-crawling sensation of how fragile life is.

Of course, too much of a good thing is bad, and too much risk would dampen the spirits of even the most ardent adventurers. So the way climbers climb is calculated to maintain a certain acceptable level of risk and uncertainty. "Style" is the word usually used to describe this process. Using an aluminum ladder to scale an indoor climbing wall, for example, would be considered "bad style." It would be too easy. But using ladders to climb the Khumbu Icefall on Everest is considered standard practice. The icefall is so dangerous you may die anyway, with or without ladders.

Attitude is also useful in maintaining an acceptable level of risk, as I realized during a bad weather stint with a climber on Kanchenjunga. We were down to two handfuls of mashed potato powder, spindrift avalanches were pummeling the twisted remains of our tent, and there was no sign of a break in the storm that had pinned us in the tent for days.

My partner was morose, convinced that we were going to have to turn around. It was true. There was no way that we could climb for three more days with only one canister of fuel to melt snow, but to enjoy the game we both needed to believe that there was some element of uncertainty in our predicament. While he burrowed deeper into his sleeping bag, I stuck my head and shoulders out of the tent to empty a pee bottle. When I pulled back inside, I nudged him and thumped my mitts together.

"Hey, guess what? Take a look outside. There's almost no wind, and I saw a break in the clouds," I announced, "I think it's gonna be calm tomorrow. Might be a good time to brew some water."

He grunted, poked his nose and one hand out of his bag, muttered an irreverent prayer to the f__ing weather gods, and unzipped the tent a few inches. Another gust immediately blasted icy shards through the crack.

"Almost no wind, huh?" he said with smug satisfaction.

"Yeah, well, it might be a little breezy *now*," I conceded, "You gotta look fast."

The mountains also shape the attitudes of the local communities. The view in many parts of Asia that children are naturally responsible, for example, is accentuated in the Himalaya. On that trek to Kanchenjunga, through the remote eastern regions of Nepal, I met a Sherpani busy building a new house for her young family. The structure mirrored the simplicity and strength of its creator—expertly carved hand-hewn beams, notched and tied together with hand-woven jute cord, cemented with walls of orange clay. Up in the open rafters of the house, one of her children, a boy of two or three years, played happily with a twig.

As I eyeballed the twenty-foot drop below the unsupervised child, I thought about devices like plastic stair gates that have presumably saved the lives of countless American children. One of the two Nepali porters who was accompanying me came up behind me.

"Isn't that dangerous?" I queried, pointing at the toddler.

The porter looked at me with confusion. Then he smiled, shook his head, and asked simply, "Why he jump?"

In the West we live in a safe and relatively comfortable world. We do everything we can to preserve and prolong our physical existence. We vaccinate our children, pass laws that mandate seat belts, develop life-saving devices like air bags and tamper-resistant packages. And we spend exorbitant amounts of energy developing products that enhance physical comfort: soft-ride suspension systems, scented fabric softeners, high-tech shoes with gel and air bubbles.

Longevity and comfort are, of course, good things. But in our quest for physical comfort, we often neglect our spiritual need to honestly and openly confront both our own mortality and the fragility of our world. We pad all of the sharp edges in our lives with bleached cotton or high-tech foam, and then wonder why the notion of a wild wind whipping across an exposed ridge both terrifies and fascinates us. We deny our kids real challenges, guarantee that they'll move from grade to grade, and then wonder why they respond with apathy and indifference. We travel to work in climate-controlled vehicles and spend the day in a gray cubicle, and then wonder why we crave caffeine and other artificial stimulants.

Deprived of risk and real danger, many people invent games that artificially create adrenaline rushes. Some of us even invent artificial problems and enemies, like psychosomatic illnesses and soap-opera relationships. In many cases, we are simply craving true challenges and real journeys, experiences in which the outcome is not certain and real loss is possible.

I stopped, suddenly realizing that my monologue was beginning to sound like a sermon.

"Sorry, I didn't mean to lecture," I said, and glanced over at Hiddle.

His legs were splayed, and he had one hand loosely draped over his thigh, head back against the seat, jaw slack.

He was asleep.

There is a gap between man's powers to conceive and his ability to achieve that can be bridged only by desire.

— KHALIL GIBRAN

FROZEN GUINNESS

When I woke up the morning after burying Maurice, the persistent grumbling in my stomach drove me out of our tent much earlier than usual. Zee and Chris were awake, too, both as hungry as I was after days of eating minimal amounts on the mountain. We ambled over to Captain Jahanzeb's tent like bears in the springtime. The captain's voice was sleepy but adamant: "No, no, thank you very much. I have tried to light the stove by myself yesterday morning, and after some very careful consideration I have come to the conclusion that it is most likely better to die of hunger than to be burned alive."

On the way to K2, we had managed to persuade the captain that the best way to prepare for his impending matrimony in September would be to learn to cook. The day before, after one solo bout with the kerosene stove in the kitchen tent, all of our painstaking work had been undone. The captain would have nothing to do with cooking or kitchens or stoves.

You see, the kerosene stoves that the cooks use at Base Camp are not ordinary stoves. They are fire-spitting dragons. They can throw flames two or three feet in the air during the priming process, and if you are not careful, they will lick the side of the kitchen tent and incinerate the entire tent and much of your facial hair in one hot puff.

Losing facial hair was not a welcome prospect, but we had decided that the risk is worth the gain. Expeditions usually employ a cook and assistant to maintain Base Camp and prepare meals while the team is recovering off the mountain and preparing for the next trip up. Our assistant cook had had to be evacuated two days earlier from the army base at Concordia for treatment of severe abdominal pains (later diagnosed as kidney stones), and our cook, Sher Afzal, had left six days earlier for an eight-day walk to retrieve a barrel of fresh food in Askole. We had persuaded one of the cooks for the Spanish team to teach us how to make chappatis (a flat, round bread) the night before, and we were now determined to test our stove-lighting, chappati-making, stomach-filling skills.

The first part was easy. Zee lit the little pool of kerosene in the well of the stove, I pushed the wall of the tent away from the stove, Zee blew the flame away. It flickered down, blue fire roared. No problem.

The second part was a little more difficult. Zee and I decided to surprise Captain Jahanzeb and his mate, Captain Atif (the liaison officer for the Italian team), with a cup of bed tea. Problem was, neither of us had ever made Pakistani chai. Still, there was a can of something in the cook tent that looked and smelled like tea, and, well, who knows? we figured. Maybe if we add it to hot water, it will make hot tea.

Zee dumped about a third of the can into a big kettle of water, and we squatted next to the kettle to wait. Suddenly one of us remembered that Pakistani chai was made with milk, too, so we rummaged through the little plastic bags arranged on the open stone floor of the kitchen tent until we found something that looked and smelled like powdered milk. Zee added a handful of it to the kettle, and *poof!* the contents of the kettle exploded, bubbling over the brim like a mad scientist's brew.

We yanked the kettle off the fire and lifted the lid to inspect the contents. *Voilà!* The outside of the kettle was covered in grinds, but the inside—well, it looked and smelled like tea. Zee poured out two cups of the concoction and brought them with a bowl of something that looked and smelled like sugar to the captains' tents. Fifteen minutes later, we heard a burst of uncontrolled laughter.

"We are accustomed to sleeping until midday, until it is warm enough to come out of our sleeping bags," the captain explained, "We have never had this thing called bed tea. It is very nice, and, well, not so nice."

Half an hour later, Zee was slapping chappati dough (a simple mixture of flour and water) in flat circles, and Chris and I were cracking eggs into a bowl. It was our turn to laugh. The eggs had been purchased almost three weeks before, in Skardu, and had traveled more than a hundred miles up the glacier with us, packed in a bed of straw. They had been subjected to wildly fluctuating temperatures. Some were rotten.

But bad eggs, we discovered, come in at least eight different categories. There are cloudy ones, gray viscous ones, neon green ones, watery puke-yellow ones, solid black ones, and the traditional moldy green sulfuric ones. Chris and I had to crack about 15 eggs to find 5 semi-acceptable ones, and by the time we reached the 15th egg we were laughing so hard we woke up an Italian climber who lived in a tent near our kitchen tent.

"You are having so much fun with no cook!" he commented.

"Almost anything is fun for one day," I responded. "But I think tomorrow it will seem like work."

Out travails were put in perspective, however, by a true tragedy suffered by the Irish team on K2 several weeks later. They had arrived at Base Camp after several weeks of climbing and acclimatizing on Broad Peak and were prepared to join us in the summit bid on K2. We had all welcomed them at Base Camp, in part because every climber within a hundred miles knew that they were brewing a barrel of beer, fermenting virgin yeast provided by Guinness, their sponsor in Dublin.

But now something was wrong.

We found one of the Irish climbers standing outside our mess tent, looking forlorn.

"We're g'win home," he announced.

The yeast for their Guinness, he explained, had frozen.

"HAVE YOU EVER BEEN TO THE GUINNESS FACTORY?" HIDDLE asked. It was 3:00 a.m., and we were looking for a place to stop. I had tried one exit, surfing the wake of a snowplow, but nothing looked open and we had hopped back on the highway.

"No. Almost all of my family is from England, so every time we go over, we seem to spend most of our time with them. I haven't been to Ireland yet. Why? Have you?"

"Yeah, I went to Dublin about three years ago to photograph birds migrating in the East Atlantic flyway. Very nutritional beer, Guinness."

I nodded. "What kind of birds?" I wanted to know.

"Arctic terns, sand martins, that sort of thing. The arctic tern population dropped a few years ago because the sand-eel population in their nesting areas was down. The sand-eel population was affected by overfishing, people think. But mostly I was interested in getting shots of whole flocks over an area called Swords. Why do you ask?"

I shrugged. "Just that migrating birds have always amazed me. The way they all move in formation, or at least so close together, without ever colliding. There's nothing in the motion of a single bird that would make you think they could circle in tight formation or fly so fluidly within inches of each other for thousands of miles. Same thing with schools of fish in the ocean."

"Mmm," he agreed.

"Do you know if there are birds that migrate at night?" I asked.

He thought for a minute. "Well, there's at least one bird—I can't remember the name of it—that migrates over Ireland at night. I remember hearing about them because they sometimes get toasted by the burning gas being flared from platforms off the coast of Cork, especially in bad weather."

"So how does it navigate?"

"I don't know. The stars, I guess."

"In bad weather?"

Hiddle laughed, "I don't know. Why?"

"Oh, I don't know. I vaguely remember hearing about these experiments with homing pigeons, where they attached magnets to them, or something like that, and it screwed up their sense of direction. They've found minute traces of magnetite in their brains, so the speculation is that they've got some kind of magnetic sense. Kind of makes you wonder if there are any senses that we have but don't know about. I mean, some kind of sensory input, like electromagnetism, that is processed on an autonomous level, without us being consciously aware of it."

The butterfly counts not months but moments,
and has time enough.

— RABINDRANATH TAGORE,
Stray Birds

METAMORPHOSIS

A gust of wind rattled the tent poles and jerked me out of a dreamless half-sleep. I looked at my watch, panicked. Four o'clock a.m. It was past time to go. Why weren't the kitchen stoves going? Why was everyone asleep?

A minute later I heard our cook, Sher, cough, and one of the kerosene stoves sputter to life. Sher and everyone else must have overslept, too. Probably just a case of collective exhaustion. I fumbled for my headlamp and silently chided myself for my negligence. We had a long day ahead of us, and we needed to start as early as possible so that we would have time to rehydrate and recover up at Camp 2.

A half hour later, though, I was pulling on my double-plastic boots, rubbing and blowing on my hands to warm them up after each tug of the laces, when I heard a tremendous *crack!* Some 3,000 feet above the glacier, a minute increase in ambient temperature with the dawn of the new day had loosened the crystalline bonds that held the slope together and triggered a massive avalanche.

A fracture line fanned across the slope of a thousand-foot-wide couloir. Thousands of tons of ice and snow and rock hurtled down the flank of K2 with the force and speed of a locomotive. I stared, slack-jawed.

By the time gravity had completed its work, the avalanche had traveled down the mountain, all the way across the Godwin-Austen Glacier, and several hundred feet up the slopes of Broad Peak, leaving a thousand-foot-high cloud of snow in its wake. It was the biggest avalanche I have ever seen anywhere.

Had we left on time, we would have been directly in its path. Sure, we wouldn't have been hit by the crushing, churning mass of snow that poured onto the lateral moraine at the edge of the glacier. We would have had time to throw ourselves down and cover our heads with our packs, so we probably would have been O.K.

As we shouldered our packs and started to move up the glacier, I couldn't help thinking this was a stroke of good fortune. Timing is everything in this world; and timing, in the end, is nothing more than luck.

We crossed the debris zone about an hour out of Base Camp. At its fringes the wind-blasted snow had a strange, polished surface, a gelatinous skin that shattered with each step like a sheet of fine crystal. I tiptoed, then danced, and finally plodded across the surface, unable to cross it without destroying it.

In the midst of this evanescent, fragile skin of snow, I spotted a small brown moth, with psychedelic orange-and-yellow swirls on its delicate wings. Wings that were encrusted in ice, frozen into the snow.

I had seen moths frozen into a glacier once before, on a peak in the Oregon Cascades. My plan was to climb by the full moon. But the moon had not yet risen above the rocky spires of the peak, and as I followed the white circle illuminated by my headlamp, I spotted first one, then another, then another brown moth embedded in the snow. A quick sweep of the headlamp across the glacier revealed hundreds of them. Hairy brown moths. Moths with a three-inch wingspan and beady black eyes. Not the kind you usually find at altitude.

What, I wondered, would entice them up to such a lonely, lifeless altitude? And why was the glacier covered with their frozen bodies? An hour later, the full moon crested the peak and answered my question. Its clear silver light, reflected off the smooth sheen of the glacier, was so bright that it must have been visible for miles. Moths are attracted to light. I could imagine them spotting the irresistible glow from several thousand feet below. I could picture them flying blindly into the luminous wall of ice, struggling to free their wings from the embrace of the snow.

On K2, as I examined the moth that had been caught in the avalanche, I was awed by the savage but tender power of the mountain. The words of another American climber, Willi Unsoeld, echoed in my mind. "When was the last time you encountered the sacred?" he asked, "the last time that your soul trembled with the indubitable awareness that it was being flooded with a numinous presence? Whatever the sacred is, it is unquestionably the most fascinating experience of our lives. It draws us almost against our will. We continue to seek it out, as the moth does the flame."

In the presence of the unpredictable forces of the mountain, we find humility. The power overwhelms our puny attempts at reason. In the face of an avalanche, the strongest of us are keenly aware that we can control only the flow of our life, and not our destiny.

As we picked our way through the debris from the avalanche and the rushing rivers of the ice flow, I stopped to watch a handful of little stones that were caught in a swirling eddy in a crystal-clear rivulet. They popped up, spun around, dancing their mad polka for a few hours each day, until the sun set and they were frozen in place again. Above the stones and my own body squatting next to the river, I noticed a gorak, a Himalayan bird of prey, spiraling up into the vaporous sky, circling on some invisible thermal. I paused, struck by the similarity between the bird's movements and the motion of the stones. That motion around a vortex is the same precise funnel shape seen in whirlpools, in tornadoes, in telescopic photos of cosmic matter swirling into a black hole.

As I WAS DRIVING, TRYING TO DESCRIBE THE MOTHS AND the pebbles and the random cyclic patterns of things. Hiddle listened, patiently, mutely munching on some pretzels. Yet, suddenly he interrupted me with a question. "What happened to Zee?"

"Zee?" I asked, caught off guard.

"Yeah. You said you were with him at one of those camps, and he dumped his oatmeal in the snow. I think you said you realized that your marriage was like the oatmeal, all sticky and frozen or something."

I had to retrace the sequence of the trip in my memory. It must have been mid-July when we found Maurice's body. It was mid-August when we went up on the final summit bid. The National Geographic TV producer, David Hamlin, had arrived at Base Camp a couple of weeks before, when we were on our first solid push to Camp 3. That was in early August. So the point at which Zee really started to lose it was somewhere around the end of July or beginning of August.

"I guess the oatmeal thing wasn't exactly an epiphany," I admitted. "There were other things that happened during the expedition that seemed more like turning points then."

There was the violence toward other climbers and the Pakistani army officers, for one. Although I didn't want to admit it to Hiddle, I had somehow convinced myself over the years that either I deserved everything that Zee had done to me, or I was capable of keeping his anger in check, and when his anger erupted it was indirectly my fault. I had somehow slipped, not read the warning signs early enough. When he directed his anger toward other individuals on K2, the onus of guilt was suddenly lifted. For the first time I saw him getting irrationally angry and violent with someone else, someone who was clearly innocent.

I decided to tell Hiddle about the mail incident.

"Toward the end of July, one of the Balti porters brought some international mail from our agent in Islamabad. There was a letter for me. It was already opened when it reached Base Camp. No big deal—the envelope was heavyweight paper, so the customs officials in Islamabad had probably decided to open it to see if it had money or something useful inside. That sort of thing happens all the time. But Zee decided to start an inquisition."

According to the accounts of other climbers who witnessed the whole thing, he brought the envelope to each of the army officers at Base Camp, asking them in an aggressive manner whether they thought the envelope should have been opened. Were they were proud of a country that violated basic rights to privacy, and what were they going to do about it? He stomped on a Pakistani army cap in a fit of temper. He got angry at Captain Jahanzeb for no apparent reason over breakfast one morning and ordered him to leave the mess tent. The captain didn't move, of course, so Zee lifted a table full of condiments and threw it on to him. Mustard, hot sauce—all of our most valuable commodities—crashed onto the stone floor of the tent. This happened in the presence of the National Geographic producer and a journalist who had come to Base Camp. "And that was mild, compared to what happened on the summit bid."

"To be fair," I added, "I think he was a little stressed. Sure, K2 is a turning point in anyone's life. But he was showing some really strange signs of stress. These mirrors, for example. He started bringing a hand mirror to the table almost every meal. He would stare at himself in it, sometimes during a conversation with Chris and Jahanzeb and me, sometimes completely on his own, oblivious to our presence. At first we thought he was getting a little obsessive about examining the changes in his face, the normal changes that take place when you lose 20 percent or so of your body weight in two months. But later in the expedition, we would make a joke or ask him a question, and he would just talk to himself in the mirror."

"Pretty weird," Hiddle agreed. "What do you think made him go nuts?"

I shrugged. "I don't know. What makes anyone lose it?"

It does not do to leave a live dragon out of your calculations, if you live near him.

— J. R. R. TOLKIEN

THE BLACK PYRAMID

"So we pushed up to Camp 3 on the Abruzzi in early August," I said.

"By the second week in August, the number of climbers had dwindled from 27 to 16," I continued, "and only 11 of us were still seriously intent on trying to reach the summit."

That climb up to Camp 3 was pure magic. Only once did I feel unbalanced, my crampons scratching across a slick, textureless granite surface. The rest of the eight hours up from Camp 2 was a dance: place, pull, up! done, search for an edge, place, stand, rest, reach, start again. The air was clean, and the dark black rock shimmered with the deep blue of the sky and the clear sparkling white reflecting off the snow. Pure magic.

Up at Camp 3, though, things were different. As I looked at the seracs towering above, I knew that the slopes were loaded. The camp was even more avalanche-prone than usual. When one of the slabs happens to cut loose, it can bury tents and the climbers who happen to be in them under several feet of snow. For this reason climbers at Camp 3 usually sleep with a knife on a string around their necks.

"Let's find a platform in the Black Pyramid," I said to Chris.

He looked mildly surprised but didn't question the decision. The Black Pyramid, you see, is not the best place on Earth to establish a camp. It is a thousand-foot region of vertical rock and ice, pocked with snow slabs and drips of ice hanging off steep ledges.

We hunted around for an hour and finally, late in the day, found a ledge about five feet wide that we figured might do.

The only hitch was that the ledge was angled at about a 50 degree angle down. Toward the glacier 4,000 feet below. What made this particular ledge so desirable was that it was *only* 50 degrees instead of the typical 80 to 90. The slope was gentle enough to actually hold snow.

After noticing that the tent was slipping a few feet every 15 minutes, and observing the obvious strain on the grommets anchoring the 3-millimeter strings to the fly of the tent, Chris and I decided to improvise a harness. There was an old purple 10-millimeter rope about 50 feet up the slope. Chris climbed up to get it, I wrapped it around the girth of the tent, and we cinched it tight with an ascender.

I once heard someone define Himalayan climbing as the "art of suffering." I understand the suffering part, but I'm not sure I fully grasp the artistic challenge. Unless he meant the sort of artistic talent that it takes to imagine that you are actually sleeping in a tent that is perched on a 50-degree angle with a fatal drop directly below. During the night I dozed off every half hour, slipped down into the trench hammock on one side of the tent, and woke up to feel Chris rhythmically tugging at my suit time after time, trying to pull me back onto our tiny ledge. "I don't know how you can sleep," he grumbled, "but you'll be sleeping a long time if the seams of this tent break and you fall 4,000 feet down to the glacier."

Several hours into the night, we decided to melt a pot of snow. This simple task quickly turned into a comedy of errors in our confined quarters. Rigging a makeshift harness around the tent had twisted it into a strange asymmetrical shape and there was almost no room for the hanging stove. Deep splits in our fingertips caused by weeks of exposure to cold made manipulating the pot grippers and gas nozzle on the stove an arduous, painful task. And then Chris slipped too close to the stove and burned a hole in his down suit.

In our oxygen-deprived state, we found the puff of down feathers that emerged from the hole in Chris' suit extremely funny. At Base Camp, I had been sporadically quoting from a book entitled *The Twins Stories: Participant Coding in Yagua Narrative*, by Thomas Edward Payne. In it are carefully recorded dialogues (with translations) that Dr. Payne observed in the community of the Yaguas, a tribe of about 3,000 people living along the Amazon River east of Iquitos, Peru.

We quoted from these dialogues whenever anything was going wrong.

On K2, our favorite phrase was *"Jatiy ji-ya muuy! Jaamu ravichu sa-kiinay Tokachiy yu-unuu-pada-mu,"* which translated as, "Don't go there! The Tokachi bird will defecate a large rock on your head!"

"I wish these feathers," Chris said, staring vacantly at the little puffs that had come out of his suit, "would morph into Tokachi eggs or something to eat."

The next morning came very slowly, like a hangover or a bad headache. We yawned, shivered, yawned again, dusted little granules of ice off the hoods of the down suits and sleeping bags.

Altitudes above 23,000 feet (7,000 meters) have a Swiss-cheese effect on my brain. There are holes in my memory. One of them is a two-hour gap somewhere between waking up and leaving camp on that morning. I can't remember exactly how we managed to melt snow without frying nylon in the remaining two-foot slot inside the tent. Or what I did with the spare pair of down mitts I had in my pack. Or where we decided to stash the tent once we somehow thawed the poles enough to get them back in the bag.

I do remember watching a particular large avalanche peel off the Shoulder. The snow came down, *whumph*, just like that, as I was squatting, emptying my bowels, hanging off the waist belt on my harness with the back flap of my suit open. I twisted around to watch the cloud explode and then dissipate at the bottom, feeling very foolish and lucky. Our sleepless night on that little ledge, I knew, had been justified. All of a sudden getting back to Base Camp seemed like a beautifully simple objective.

Climbing back down, we had a constant clear view of the fresh fan of snow on the glacier almost a mile below.

THE NEXT WEEK BROUGHT DAY AFTER DAY OF MISERABLE weather. "Monsoon weather here!" Captain Jahanzeb announced one morning as he burst into the mess tent for breakfast. His voice had a slightly too happy overtone that suggested that he knew what happens to mountaineering expeditions when the monsoon weather arrives.

I glared at him. "No such luck, Captain," I growled. "We're here for at least another 20 days, and I'll add 5 to that for every time you even mention the monsoon."

It was snowing, no, sleeting outside, and the low-lying clouds and general moodiness of the weather had produced a state of mass restlessness at Base Camp. There had been no climbers on the mountain since our descent from Camp 3, and the short-wave radio broadcasts being intercepted by the Brazilian climber Waldemar Niclevicz were reporting epic floods in the Bay of Bengal and unusual weather patterns elsewhere in the globe that were being attributed to El Niño. No one wanted to admit it, but we all knew that the conditions high on the mountain would probably prevent us from reaching the summit.

Even if we went ahead and climbed up to Camp 3 in miserable weather, even if the weather gave us a 48-hour window to get from Camp 3 to the summit and back, we still faced the problem of the depth of the accumulated snow on the Shoulder. This area of the route is a broad, open terrace of snow. Although the wind that whips over the ridge sometimes packs the snow into a hard, firm base, it more often deposits deep, irregular drifts on top of avalanche-prone wind-slab snow.

The Shoulder lies in the 7,000- to 8,000-meter zone. It is difficult enough just to climb at that altitude, especially without supplemental oxygen. To shovel your way through thigh- or chest-deep drifts is impossible. The conditions had already been bad on our first trip up. Now there was another week's worth of heavy snow.

On August 9 came a break, a shift in the wind that signaled a possible weather window. Not a big break, but the 11 of us who were still hanging out at Base Camp scrambled to get ready. I put on clean underwear, brushed my teeth. Carefully packed the picture of my daughter, the shark's teeth, and other little trinkets I wanted to carry to the summit just in case.

We climbed directly to Camp 2 and spent a few frozen hours melting more snow, rehydrating, and nervously watching the clouds building on the southeastern horizon. We made plans with other climbers to synchronize our departure times so that we could share the work of breaking trail to the summit.

The final summit bid on an 8,000-meter peak is both an intensely personal and integrally connected affair. Each climber sets out knowing that he is ultimately responsible for anything that happens to him. When something starts to go wrong, though, you suddenly find yourself working with other climbers, bound by powerful ties of compassion. A tent explodes in high winds, and you find space for another body in your tent. A partner is snowblind, and you guide her down. The route is obscured by blowing snow and clouds, and you leave one of your poles to mark the top of the fixed lines.

At least this is what happens when things go only slightly wrong.

If things go seriously wrong—if someone has pulmonary edema, or a cerebral embolism, or any of the other incapacitating altitude-related problems, or if the weather suddenly disintegrates—the game suddenly becomes a solo endeavor again.

As I climbed, I thought about the other people on the mountain. Everyone seemed strong, but Chris and I had been the only climbers who had managed to snag an opportunity to spend a night above 23,000 feet (7,000 meters) before the final push to

28,250 feet (8,611 meters). What would happen once we all pushed ourselves up above 26,000 feet (8,000 meters) without bottled oxygen?

We were each alone, completely alone, I reminded myself.

As I climbed though, I didn't feel alone; I felt overwhelmed, crowded by voices in the air. They were a buzzing sort of presence, and it was as though every breath I took was saturated with invisible swarming spirits.

"HOLD ON A SEC, I'VE GOTTA FIX THAT WINDOW." I PAUSED at this point in the story to inch the car over into the breakdown lane, jump out, and roll up the window on the rear passenger seat, driver's side. We had just driven over a series of frost heaves and little ridges in the plowed snow. I had bought the car—the Beast, I called it—for a slide show tour around New England, hoping to get a few thousand miles out of it before it quit. It was old and crotchety, and the window had a quirky habit of slipping out of the track and sliding down a couple of inches if you hit a speed bump or a pothole just wrong. Normally it was no big deal to just roll the window back up. But right now the handle seemed to be frozen solid, and no matter how much I rattled it and pounded the door, I couldn't get it or the window to budge. The snow must have gotten down into the gap between the window and the frame, and sealed the handle in place.

Hiddle watched my antics with an amused kind of detachment, obviously deep in thought about something. I finally settled for stuffing an old towel into the crack, and clambered back into the driver's seat.

"My uncle," he began as we slid back onto the highway, "he was a bee farmer. He had a dozen or so apiaries in his orchard, and when we were kids he used to let the bees crawl all over him. He probably would've understood that feeling that you were just talking about. You know, what did you call it? A swarming kind of feeling."

I started to laugh. I couldn't help it.

"No, I'm not kidding," he persisted. "He used to tell us this story about the bees and the jungle. He used to say that underneath the bees, his skin felt like it was crawling, like a pile of snakes, and under the snakes, he could feel the little bites of red ants, and under the ants, there was the buzzing of the green flies, and so on. The thing that bothered him was all the writhing and crawling and slithering, the sheer volume of all the life."

There's no life in the upper reaches of the atmosphere—at least no buzzing, biting, crawling life—but there was something about Hiddle's connection that made sense. In the jungle, there is a certain sort of torpor, a certain seething, humid indifference that fills you with terror. The kind of terror that creeps up on you like the long woody vines that coil around the ankles of the trees. The jungle is green, green, everywhere green, and the humming and shrieking and hissing can overwhelm the senses.

On a mountain, there is something about the sheer *lack* of life that is repugnant, baleful, invidious. Climbing, oh so slowly climbing up a long, frozen slope of snow and ice, you know you are an intruder, a trespasser in a world of beauty that is not meant for living, breathing things. A wall of granite springs up out of the snow in front of you, baring twisted dikes of malevolent black rock, contorted scars from the proterozoic period. You sink into the slope up to your waist, and the snow underneath you gives way to reveal a hidden crevasse, a dark, bottomless chasm lined with glistening teeth of ice. Above is only a faceless, flat sky, pressing down.

FIVE DAYS AFTER WE LEFT BASE CAMP FOR THE FINAL summit bid, we were nowhere near the top. We were still at Camp 2, getting ready to go back down. The wind was pounding like a hammer, driving nails of ice into the walls of our tent. One of the other climbers, Waldemar Niclevicz, flopped down in the snow outside our tent. Zee and I unzipped the door to offer him hot liquids, and found him grinning behind his goggles, his smile framed by an ice-encrusted mustache and beard.

I groaned. I was upset about the weather, about the prospect of carrying inhumanly heavy loads back to Base Camp, about the waist-deep wet white stuff up on the Shoulder that made reaching the summit a schoolchild's fantasy.

"Waldemar," I demanded, "why are you so happy?"

His disgustingly cheery smile went from ear to happy ear. "This year," he announced in a rich, serene, mature voice, "K2 is impossible. Now I know I will go home, eat a *lot*, and come back again next year."

Pepe Garçes, his Spanish partner, echoed a similar sentiment. "In 1995 the weather was bad and so many climbers died. This year the weather is much worse, and the snow is bad. It's time to go home."

As I stared at the swirling mass of clouds on the slopes above, I knew he was right. Despite heavy snowfall for the previous two weeks, there had been no big avalanche to clear the dangerous slopes above the Black Pyramid. Even the very high winds had not compacted the snow, and more snow was being dumped every day. There were inverted thermals, too, with low-lying clouds that signaled the premature onset of the monsoon.

No one had reached the summit. No one would, that year or the next. In some years K2 is impossible.

As I said, the final commitment to climb any mountain is both an intensely personal and an intricately connected decision. Each climber not only risks her own life but also accepts a deep responsibility toward other climbers, family, and friends. I resolved in that moment to pack our bags and start hauling gear down. In some ways, it was an easy decision.

THE CLIMBING WAS DONE, BUT THE EVENTS THAT WOULD embed themselves in our minds forever were only just starting.

Was it the disappointment of not reaching the summit that kindled the anger smoldering in Zee's eyes? Or was it a nagging sense of loss, the feeling that his past and his future were slipping like rivulets of water through his fingers?

Whatever it was, I wasn't oblivious to the turbulence in his emotions. The tension in our tent, for no discernable reason, was as thick as the swirling fog that obscured the sun. I placated him, added sweeteners to everything I said, stepped lightly, afraid of our shattered dreams. "Tea or hot chocolate?" I asked. "Do you want something to eat? Cheese? Salami?"

The first eruption occurred early the next morning, a stormy dawn at Camp 2. One of the Turkish climbers was in the tent facing ours, with Chris, recovering from exhaustion and dehydration so severe that there he had blood in his urine. I had given him my sleeping bag the night before, and Chris had been slowly feeding him liquids all night. I stepped across the two-foot boundary between our tents, into the tent where Chris and the Turk were melting snow, preparing to descend. I must have stayed too long.

"Heidi?!" I heard Zee shouting from the other tent.

"Just a minute," I answered. "The stove is on, I can't get out until it's done."

An angry hand unzipped the other tent, unzipped the door of the tent we were huddled in, reached in and grabbed my collar. Chris jerked the pot of melting snow to the side of the tent, yanked the propane/butane cartridge and the flame away from my clothing, and the hand dragged me back into its domain.

Zee and I didn't say anything to each other back in our tent. I pretended nothing had happened. We silently packed, getting ready to return to Base Camp.

I had learned the art of pacification, of conceding, of not caring.

The fire of the stove hadn't burned me, but the sun was about to.

Up until then the sun had been a mere memory, a yellow muffled reflection of the moon hidden behind a white river of clouds. Somehow it escaped that day.

Heading out into the storm, descending from Camp 2, Zee refused to go first. He didn't want to be filmed. Didn't want to film. Chris and I reluctantly descended ahead of him. I could see the warning signs, the molten lava in his eyes.

I didn't stop to wonder why he was angry. Reasons didn't seem to matter. Avalanches and volcanoes are facts of nature. You don't ask why. They just happen.

The terrain between Camp 2 and Camp 1 is full of large, loose rocks. Chris was hit on the head. I ducked, was hit on the thigh and back of my pack. We clung to the rope and tumbled down as fast as gravity would carry us.

At Camp 1, 3,000 feet below, we paused to take off our down suits. Members of the Italian team shouted at Chris and me. One of the rocks had hit their tents. Chris shrugged and shook his head. I tried to apologize.

The orb in the sky was emerging from the clouds, about to blaze down and singe our nerves.

When Zee arrived, Chris shook his head again. He had just peeled the crampons off his boots and was starting to take off his over-boots. "It's a good thing we're getting off this mountain before someone gets killed," he remarked casually, more to himself than anyone else.

"What," Zee demanded, "did you just say?"

"I said," Chris repeated, still calm, "that it's a good thing we're getting off this mountain before someone gets killed."

Zee picked up an ice axe and flew at Chris. Chris grabbed the rope and slithered down the steep slope below Camp 1, slipping without his crampons on. Zee started to hack at the rope with the axe. I grabbed him from behind, around the neck, trying to wrestle him away from the rope. He turned on me with the axe, incredulous, started to swing again, and then stopped. Chris somehow managed to scramble up the rope, grab his pack, and head down the ropes on the other side of the camp, rappelling in a frenzy of motion and fear. I dragged Zee into our remaining tent at Camp 1, breathing too hard to talk, trying not to cry. Distractedly, I noticed the puff of feathers bleeding from the arm of my suit.

Beyond myself

                somewhere

        I wait for my arrival.

—OCTAVIO PAZ,
The Balcony

THE GONDOGORO LA

I glanced over at Hiddle after I finished the story. I tried to imagine the thoughts running through his mind. I waited for him to ask an obvious, safe, neat little question. Why did you do this, or why didn't you do that? But instead he just shook his head.

"Wow," he said, "I can't believe he was so ineffective."

"What do you mean?"

"Well, I mean, if you wanted to kill someone on K2, it would be easy enough to do, wouldn't it?"

I shrugged. "Nothing was that premeditated," I responded. "It wasn't as though he was deliberately threatening Chris or other climbers or me." At least it didn't seem that way to me; he didn't threaten me until after the expedition, until we were back home, I reminded myself.

In some ways the events of those next two weeks were predictable, a necessary series of aftershocks that allowed the trembling
earth to settle after the eruption.

Is there a force, a law of nature that hurls things apart? What
primeval energy makes volcanoes explode, lightning fork, and trees
branch? Our universe is ever more complex, flung across the reaches
of space, growing, fragmenting into ever smaller units of truth. It was
this way of the world that we experienced during those two weeks.

Things diverged. Things separated. Things fell apart.

I PACKED IN A FRENZY OF MOTION. THERE WERE CHECKLISTS
and dozens of identical plastic barrels that allowed me to divvy our
stuff up into separable, containable units. Extra fuel in one barrel,
rope in another, medical supplies in yet another—mark it with a
big cross of duct tape, I reminded Chris. I ran through quantities
and logistics like an automaton. Put film in a waterproof case. Mark
that duffel of extra food so that we remember to give it to the porters
at the end of the trek. Lock the barrel of trash so it doesn't get
dumped on the glacier. Tape up the adze and pick of each axe. Don't
forget to pull out another digital video cassette; we need to shoot
some more footage of the Gilkey Memorial for National Geographic
on the way out.

What, I wonder now, was the glue holding everything together?
Was it fear or relief that impelled me forward?

Chris was also coolly rational and logical, though still afraid. "The
absolute and pure brutality of that attack," he wrote in his journal,
alone in a hotel room in Bangkok two weeks later, "will stay with
me forever. The realization that there is an explosive violence and

naked brutality that can be hidden in a person and all of a sudden triggered, like a gun, is what terrified me much more than the physical violence. The wounds of fear are worse than the injuries from the crampons on my leg and the ice axe on my hands and arms. Skin heals in two weeks and mostly doesn't leave any signs of memory except maybe a scar. The body is able to heal and forget, the mind is not. At least mine is not."

Upset by the events on the mountain, he refused to trek out with Zee. Captain Jahanzeb consulted with the other liaison officers at Base Camp. They were still angry about the incidents with the army cap and the breakfast table. Arrest him in Islamabad, one L.O. suggested. Not a good solution, another argued; too much paperwork. There were two possible routes out of Base Camp. They discussed combinations of dividing us up, arranging us, and shipping us out.

I tried to dredge up everything I knew about the law in Pakistan, which wasn't much. Showing disrespect by stomping on the army cap, I suspected, was the worst crime Zee had committed. Pakistani law is based on English common law, a legacy of colonialism, but in 1979 the government decided to establish a religious court in accordance with Islamic law. The new changes included the death penalty for defiling the name of the Prophet Muhammad, stoning for adultery and fornication, amputation of hands or feet for crimes against property, and flogging for public drunkenness. Although flogging is occasionally carried out, the death penalty and amputations are usually reversed on appeal.

Significant differences exist in the enforcement of the law for men and for women. In the case of rape, for example, men are rarely found guilty because four Muslim males of good reputation must appear as witnesses to the act. If the man is acquitted, then the woman who has brought the charge can be punished for adultery or admitting to an illicit sexual act. In the case of "blood money," the money that a victim's family can demand from a perpetrator in lieu of inflicting equivalent harm, only half the amount must be paid if the victim is female.

I assumed there were also significant differences for Pakistanis and for foreigners, but I didn't want to ask. In the end, the captain decided that Zee and our assistant cook should go down the Baltoro Glacier with half of the loads. Chris, our cook, the captain, and I would go out over the alternate route, the Gondogoro La.

Zee at first refused, then suddenly agreed, and left Base Camp one morning with a sleeping bag and a pack full of basic supplies. I hugged him before he left.

Left alone at Base Camp, I didn't bother to divide up our belongings. They were already crumbling into little useless pieces. I knew he wouldn't want anything when we got home.

By the time the porters from the villages in the Shegar Valley arrived, the day after we had finished hauling all of our equipment down from the mountain and packing up Base Camp, I had resolved to sift through the fragments that were mine, to piece together a coherent mosaic out of the shattered bits of memories, a stained glass window of the past that would be whole again, even if I wasn't. When you're young, you think everything can be pieced together again. You think you can reshape and refigure yourself and the past, pulling together the parts you want to remember and discarding the rest. You don't yet know that the past etches itself permanently in the little crevices on your face, the way the future is etched in your hands.

As we watched the porters tying loads together, the captain smiled and rubbed his hands together. He was in a gleeful, almost exuberant mood. "We shall be home, *Inshallah*, in seven, maybe eight days," he announced to no one in particular.

"Easy for you to say," I responded. His confidence that the whole business was now at an end irritated me. For me, the cracks were spreading, widening under my feet. I was determined to hold it together, but somehow I knew that the worst was yet to come.

"MY AUNT," HIDDLE INTERRUPTED SUDDENLY, "LIVED IN Riyadh for a while."

I looked over at him, surprised. My aunt happened to live in Riyadh for a while, too, while my uncle worked for a British company with offices in Saudi Arabia. This struck me as a bizarre coincidence, but I didn't say anything.

"There was a Saudi Arabian woman educated in France that my aunt met through some friends in the compound she lived in. This woman was incarcerated for a sex crime that she hadn't committed. Her husband accused her of sleeping with a lover from another village, or something like that. He was the one with a lover, and he wanted to get rid of her."

I raised my eyebrows and nodded. A familiar story.

"There was some human rights organization that thought they were doing the right thing and hired a lawyer to argue her case. The tribunal decided she was innocent and released her. But she didn't want to leave the prison. They finally shipped her back to her village, completely against her will. And she was murdered there."

I nodded again. The decisions of the gavel are sterile, but the world is not. The woman's crime, or mistake, was probably returning to her village after receiving an education abroad, and attempting to integrate the divergent cultures. Sometimes, once the borders have been crossed, it is best not to go back.

"Ironic fate," Hiddle said.

LESS THAN A WEEK AFTER WE LEFT K2 BASE CAMP, WE encountered our own instance of ironic destiny on a mountain pass the Pakistanis call the Gondogoro La. Chris, the captain, our cook Sher Afzal, and I were traveling with a group of 30 porters. The ascending side of the La is a snow field in the shadow of a stack of seracs two stories high. The other side is a 30-degree slope of black metamorphic rock that can become slick in the frequent cold fog and drizzling icy rain. It is a short trek, no more than six hours from Ali Camp, on the glaciated side of the pass, to the green pastures and river to the west. Groups typically leave from Ali Camp between 2:00 and 4:00 a.m. to reduce the chance of breaking through snow bridges and falling into a crevasse or getting caught in an avalanche once the sun hits the slopes.

I knew the pass was dangerous. Several people are killed there every year. I had crossed the La in 1996 with Iñaki and swore never to lead porters over it again. But here I was, a mere two years later, crossing it with another group of men, tempting fate.

On August 23, it was snowing, blowing cold. We woke up at Ali Camp, on the snow side of the La, at midnight, and consulted in a concert of flashing, swinging headlamps. No, the snow was too heavy, and the porters were in cotton clothing. Better to wait, we all agreed, and crawled back into our tents.

On August 24, at the same time, same place, another conference of swinging headlamps was held. The snow had stopped. The stars were out, an audience of eyes in a black sky, watching the inevitable unfold. I agreed to lead, to break trail across the crevassed glacier and up the La. Chris would be the "sweep," hanging back behind the last porter in the column to make sure everyone crossed the gap safely.

We left at 2:00 a.m., and two hours later, I was halfway up the La, waiting for the column of porters below me to catch up.

Suddenly, one of the seracs on the side of the slope sagged and then slipped and broke under the weight of new snow. I watched it in slow motion, dimly comprehending what was about to happen, and then turned around, in disbelieving slow motion.

"Run! Run!" My shouts were hoarse, choked, stupid, and useless, whipped away by the wind and drowned in the roar of the avalanche. A two-story cliff of ice at the edge of the pass had just cracked and crumbled under the weight of new snow, sending a churning wave of snow and ice down the slope. It was traveling too fast to outrun, and in a moment it would engulf the column of porters and climbers standing still a hundred feet below me.

The wave hit a crest in the slope, exploded upward like surf hitting a rock, and the line instantly dispersed in a frenzy of ant-like movements. I stopped shouting, my mind unwillingly recalling the sensations of being buried in the avalanche on Kanchenjunga.

I moved as close as I dared to the edge of the slope. Chris was lost somewhere in the turmoil below. I felt a flash of disbelief. We had come too far, endured too much fear, to be separated by death.

But the wave consumed first one running body, then another. I watched carefully, mentally marking the positions. When the crushing mass of detritus ground to a stop and the surprised cries of the survivors subsided, my stomach was knotted in anguish. I knew men were dying in the snow below me. I just didn't know how many.

I threw my pack down, grabbed an axe, and started picking my way back down the hollow sheet of snow that was left clinging to the slope. An image of woven thatches of gauze floated in front of my eyes. The first-aid kit. That medical barrel with the cross of tape—where was it? At the bottom of the debris pile were two lone figures: Chris and Matt, an American who had been traveling with a Dutch group right behind us. They were chopping the ice with their axes, trying to free a porter who was buried under a pile of heavy blocks.

A quick glance at Chris's contorted face told me that he was injured. I joined them in hacking and pulling out several huge chunks of ice. A few minutes later we had succeeded in freeing the porter, a man named Ali Muhammed, from the village of Shegar. He was wide-eyed with fear, shivering in his thin, wet cotton clothes, and bleeding from wounds on his forehead and forearm. Two weeks later, we would learn that his injuries were fatal.

Just beyond Ali was a blue expedition barrel, lying in a patch of crusty snow stained red with blood.

"I don't know whose blood that is," Chris said, staring at me through eyes dilated with shock. "There was a porter under there, but he managed to free himself and ran back with the porters from the Dutch trekking group."

All of our porters had fled past me, up the hill to the top of the pass.

"Is anyone else buried?" We looked at each other and knew the answer. We just didn't know where to start. The pile of debris was 150 feet across, 20 feet deep in places. Some of the chunks of ice were as large as a car.

The guide from the Dutch group was shouting at Matt, telling him to return to the previous camp. "Another avalanche, another avalanche will come," he kept saying.

"Come on, let's look quickly," I said to Chris and Matt. "We need to get up to the top before the sun hits the slope, and we need to get Ali out of here."

We started to scramble over the debris. Several yards beyond the abandoned barrel, Matt found a hand sticking out of the snow. The body attached to the hand was buried under heavy blocks of ice. None of us knew exactly how much time had passed since the avalanche hit, but we knew it didn't matter once we had dragged the body out from under the ice. His eyes were dark blue pools of blood, and his abdomen was bloated. He was dead. The medical barrel had been on his back.

The porter was Inayat Muhammed from the village of Dasso, the cousin of our *sardar* (lead porter), Salman Ali.

Slowly, we inched our way up to the top of the pass, methodically placing boot above weary boot in the still unstable snow.

At the top we discovered the rest of the porters who had been traveling with us, huddled in a mass. They greeted Ali with hugs and kisses.

I approached Salman and Captain Jahanzeb. "How many people are missing?" I asked.

"Three," Salman responded, looking at me with wide, disbelieving eyes.

"One porter," I told them, "has gone back with the Dutch group. I'm not sure who it was. Another is dead. We covered the body with a shawl. I took a still photograph with the video camera. You can look at it at the bottom, so you know who it was."

They nodded silently.

"We left two barrels and a duffel bag nearby," I continued. "I took the satellite phone and some of the supplies from the medical kit. We can call for a helicopter for Ali on the other side."

No one was sure what to do or say. The top of the pass was cold and windy. It had started to snow, and our brains and hands were numb. Later I discovered that many of the porters were so terrified by the avalanche that they wanted to leave the barrels at the top of the pass, climb down without risking further injuries, and go home. Captain Jahanzeb somehow persuaded them to stay.

I began to fix the ropes down the steep, rocky western side of the pass. Chris followed, trying to move rocks to create footholds for the porters behind us.

The climb down was a long, laborious process. Chris, I discovered, had been tossed and twisted in the avalanche, finally landing with the crampons on his feet caught in his pack. He had a huge hematoma on his leg and a back injury, and his movements were painfully slow as he used his trekking poles to absorb the weight. We moved silently, each in our own world.

Somewhere in the apron of loose rocks near the bottom of the pass, we stumbled on a purple flower, a fragile, beautiful thing growing in the middle of a circle of precariously perched rocks. It was the first green thing we had seen in two months. I felt a flash of warmth on my cheeks and looked away, embarrassed. I don't usually cry. But when I looked back at Chris, his eyes were wet, too.

THE MYSTERY OF DEATH RUNS A TANGLED BUT POWERFUL course through the veins of life. Several hours later I was squatting next to Salman, drawing a crude diagram with a rock in the dirt of where we left Inayat's body so that he could return with men from the village and arrange an appropriate burial.

Inayat was deaf. Two days earlier he and Salman had had an argument via jerky, angry gestures about whether he should accompany us over the Gondogoro La. Salman had wanted him to go with the porters who were carrying some of our loads down the Baltoro Glacier, a longer but safer route. Inayat had refused. Only ten weeks before, we had passed through their village, Dasso. Inayat was an only son, the only source of income, for a family of nine children. Although he was deaf, he managed to support his elderly parents, his eight sisters, his wife, and his two-year-old by working as a porter during the annual May through September climbing season.

I wondered if Salman was asking himself "what if?"

Squatting next to us, the captain shook his head. "One of Inayat's cousins told me that they believe death knows no place," he explained, "when it is time, it calls you strongly, or it finds you, wherever you are."

Lying on my back in our tent that night, I thought again about that silent argument between Salman and his cousin. Why had Inayat wanted to travel via the harder route across the pass? What had fueled his stubborn resistance to the dictates of reason? Had death found him, or "called him strongly?"

What is this force that tempts us to our fate?

IN THE PROCESS OF USING THE SATELLITE PHONE TO CONTACT our agent in Islamabad and notify him that we might need a helicopter evacuation for Ali and Chris, Captain Jahanzeb discovered that the political situation in the world around us was beginning to crumble.

A helicopter rescue, we were told, would be impossible. He didn't explain why at the time. I was vaguely aware that something had happened, but I was preoccupied with trying to help Chris limp through the remaining three days of the trek. We had cleaned and stitched up a wound on Ali's forehead, and we were monitoring him for shock and signs of infection or internal injuries. Chris had a dinner-plate-size bruise on his thigh, and muscles seizing in his back, but there was no loss of sensation in his extremities or other signs of a pinched nerve. (Ali died two weeks later in a hospital in Skardu. Chris survived and was treated for back problems at home in Switzerland.)

It was a long three days.

By the time we reached Skardu, the captain was noticeably skittish. I thought of asking him why but then decided not to. I had other things on my mind.

"There has been some political unrest," is all he said. "Zee will fly to Islamabad when he arrives, and we'll drive. We'll go tonight. If we're stopped, don't say anything. I will answer the questions. Heidi, you should wear your shalwar kameez and keep your hair covered. I think I'll say you're Canadian."

There probably wouldn't be any problem, but it would be better to err on the side of caution, he explained. Chris and I just looked at each other with raised eyebrows and shrugged.

We sorted through the loads again, found the remainder of the ropes, and gave them to Salman. He would sell them in Skardu, after we left, to raise money to support Inayat's family through the winter while they waited for the insurance money from the government to come.

Less than ten hours after arriving in Skardu, we left for Islamabad.

Sometime in the middle of the night, the driver of our van pulled over to relieve himself. The road seemed deserted. Chris and Captain Jahanzeb were sleeping. I hopped out and started to walk along the edge of the road, looking for a bush to duck behind. Before I could find a spot that would be shielded from headlights, the driver came running, waving his arms and shouting. He didn't want me out of the vehicle.

I climbed back into the van, thinking uncharitable thoughts, wondering how he expected me to ride with a full bladder for fifteen hours. It took me a half hour of stealthy and precarious movements in the rollicking back seat to discreetly relieve myself in a pee bottle without removing the shalwar kameez. And it was another half an hour before the situation began to seem even vaguely amusing.

Back in Islamabad, we finally discovered what the fuss was all about.

On August 7, the U.S. embassies in Kenya and Tanzania had been bombed, killing 224 people, including 12 Americans, and injuring 5,000. The bombings had reportedly been sponsored by Osama bin Laden, a multimillionaire Islamic extremist living in Afghanistan under the protection of the Taliban. Bin Laden also allegedly financed the 1993 World Trade Center bombing in New York, through his organization Al Qaeda, which accepts applications for "religious grants." In a television interview with ABC in June, he had said "We believe that the biggest thieves in the world are Americans, and the biggest terrorists on Earth are the Americans. The only way for us to defend against these assaults is by using similar means. We do not differentiate between those dressed in military uniforms and civilians. They're all targets in this *fatwah*."

The U.S. had responded to the bombings in Africa by making retaliatory strikes against Al Qaeda sites in Sudan and Afghanistan. Violence has a way of breeding violence. The missiles destined for Afghanistan, according to Pakistani papers, had been launched across Pakistani air space without prior notice or permission. Some reports even suggested that one of the missiles had accidentally landed on Pakistani soil. (Both of these allegations were later retracted.) Anti-American rallies attended by thousands of Islamic fundamentalists were held in cities throughout Pakistan. American flags and effigies of President Clinton were being burned by angry mobs in the streets.

The U.S. had offered a five-million-dollar reward for bin Laden's capture. Bin Laden, in return, in advertisements in various Pakistani newspapers, was offering a 50,000-dollar reward for the death of any American citizen in Pakistan.

And an article in an Islamabad paper, *The Nation*, had reported the date our "American" team was due to return from K2.

Our tickets to return home were not scheduled for another three weeks.

All of the flights for the next three weeks were completely booked.

After burying the body of French climber Maurice Barrard on K2, in 1998, the line between life and death seemed impossibly thin. I imagined each one of the climbers around me vanishing. The risk seemed to have a new presence; it walked with us.

The Black Pyramid on the south side of K2 is a 1,000-foot-high region of near-vertical mixed rock and ice. The question of whether ladders and other climbing aids are acceptable can be the subject of intense debate.

To prevent the tent
from slipping to the
glacier 4,000 feet
below, we wrapped an
old rope around the
girth and cinched it
tight with an ascender.

Inayat Muhammad insisted on crossing the Gondogoro La with us, despite objections from his cousin, Salman Ali. We found his body under crushing blocks of ice and snow.

We tried to treat Ali Muhammad for shock and other injuries, but were unable to save his life. "Death has no time or place," one of our Pakistani porters remarked after the tragedy. "It finds you, wherever you are."

Our team's photographer, Bobby Model, adds a new twist to climbing through the Khumbu Icefall on Everest by using the "Model Monkey" technique to cross the ladder spanning the crevasse just below Camp 1.

"A wild labyrinth of ice-walls, chasms and towers," Eric Shipton wrote of his 1951 foray into the Khumbu Icefall. Fifty years later, it is still a challenge to find a viable route through the ever-shifting maze of debris.

To climb on the north side of K2 requires an expensive and lengthy eight-day approach, with camels, over the Aghil Pass and through the Shaksgam Valley. No helicopter rescues are available in this remote region of China, and retreat from Base Camp is almost impossible once the rivers in the Shaksgam region are in flood.

The Gilkey Memorial, a five-foot-high cairn near Base Camp, is a testimony to the savage indifference of K2. The second highest and one of the most remote peaks on Earth, K2 has either claimed the lives or exacted a high price from all of the women and many of the men who have tried to reach its 8,611-meter summit.

The American embassy was closed.

We moved from hotel to hotel, evading the media and watching armed guards outside vigilantly surveying the streets with mirrors to check for snipers under parked vehicles. I wrapped myself in a shalwar kameez and went to the airline offices every day. We used the satellite phone to call relatives and friends. Finally, after a week, we found seats on a flight from Islamabad to Karachi to Dubai to London to New York.

I HAD ONE LAST HURDLE BEFORE WE ARRIVED HOME.

Zee was on the same flight, and he wanted the film, the 35 mm film and the National Geographic footage that we had shot on the expedition.

The footage belonged to National Geographic. I contemplated simply giving it to him in a moment of apathy and then decided that no, I had a responsibility to fulfill our contract. Zee would almost certainly destroy it.

What do you do when you are alone and outside the realm of any familiar legal system, with someone who is bigger and stronger than you, and wants something you have?

I lied and told him that Chris had taken the film back to Switzerland.

And then, during a change of flight in Heathrow, London, the airport security suddenly decided to x-ray our bags again. The film was clearly visible in the bottom of my bag.

Zee chased me down the runway to the plane, shouting all the way. I laughed because it seemed more appropriate than crying and dodged into the first available single seat, in the middle of a row jammed with other passengers.

The plane took off, and I sank into the seat in a sweat of relief, still laughing and shaking and crying. I couldn't believe I'd finally be on American turf in less than seven hours. The flight would be a brief reprieve, and then all I'd have to do would be to get within sight of customs officers at the JFK airport in New York. He wouldn't do anything to me in front of airport police.

I shoved the pack with the film under my feet, pulled a blanket up over my shoulders.

The guy next to me, I noticed, was staring at me. "Do you mind if I turn the light on?" he asked.

"No, that's fine," I answered, yawning and trying to pretend to be extremely sleepy.

"Are you a Christian?" he asked.

I nodded, not in the mood for an evaluation of religious heritage and beliefs.

"Do you want to listen to some Christian music?" he asked. His voice had a pleasant sort of country western twang, and with his long sandy hair he reminded me of a rooster. Authentic and annoying.

"Sure," I said, because it seemed like the right thing to say.

He introduced himself as Don, a composer of Christian music. I listened to the music until I fell asleep. It was good music. It was good to be sitting next to someone without wondering whether he wanted to harm me.

AT THE AIRPORT, ZEE HANDED ME HIS WEDDING RING AND walked away.

I filed for divorce the next morning.

If you gaze long enough into the
abyss, the abyss gazes also into you.

— FRIEDRICH NIETZSCHE

NON SEQUITURS

"I haven't seen Zee since then," I added, almost as an afterthought.

"So are you divorced?" Hiddle wanted to know.

I shook my head, "Not yet. There's a three-month waiting period."

He nodded and shifted his weight from one bony hip to another.

I felt an involuntary surge of resentment and irritation again. When we arrived home in September, I had had mixed emotions about the expedition and getting divorced. My actions, my words were non sequiturs. Nothing seemed to follow. Nothing made sense. Eddies of cause and effect were choppy, unpredictable. Events didn't flow naturally from one to the next.

Some days that autumn I felt like a child with a boundless sense of the possible, happily flying through space on a playground swing. I could be anything, do anything, reinvent my world and maybe even my past.

On other days I felt like a crazy old woman with spidery hair, tending a garden of decaying dreams.

I was living in a four-generation household, with my 6-year-old daughter Devi, my parents, and my 82-year-old grandmother from Britain.

I started to read the first Harry Potter book to Devi in October. Were there any werewolves on K2? she wanted to know. I kissed her and told her no, nothing quite that interesting. Avalanches and mountaineering are very mundane topics when compared with ferocious three-headed dogs and a sport that you play on flying broomsticks.

My grandmother was concerned about the fact that the window in my bedroom wouldn't open. How would I air out my bed sheets? she fretted. I kissed her, too, and told her not to worry. After living in a sleeping bag for three months, the problem of un-aired bed linens struck me as about as worrisome as the unrestrained growth of plastic flowers.

I drifted through each day in apathy, with no concentration. Visions of climbing and K2 drifted through my mind like chimeras, weaving in and out of daily events. I watched them, mute. Answers to questions, mine and others,' were just out of reach. Words would not stay in place. They slipped, slid, and perished under the weight of the memories. Even the memories, I knew, would eventually decay with imprecision.

I went for long runs while Devi was at school, trying to refocus. I made a spinach casserole one night for dinner, reasoning that green leafy veggies would be good for replenishing iron reserves after three months of nutritional deprivation. Good for nutrition maybe, but not for the bowels. My guts were still slowly adapting to the richness of western food.

On the post-spinach-casserole run the next morning, I had to pause and duck behind a rock. Just as I was about to emerge, shame-faced and thoroughly grumpy, I heard the raucous sound of a group of schoolchildren.

Out on a forced march to collect snatches of falling color, no doubt. Little bits of time that would be neatly pressed and ironed in between sheets of wax paper.

This is supposed to be a *wilderness*, I groaned to myself, crouching motionless in the dry leaves as the pack of whooping little aborigines tromped past. It took them an eternity, and all the while I held my breath and clutched my hair. I felt miserable, woefully deviant and undercivilized.

I think I wished them spinach for dinner.

Later that same day, I was standing in line at the grocery store when a woman with curly red hair leaned toward me. "Hey," she said, sounding surprised, "aren't you the mountain climber?"

I contemplated saying no. Privacy, like freedom, is something that has to be claimed. Then I noticed the freckle-nosed kid standing in front of her, peering curiously at the pint of Ben and Jerry's Chunky Monkey ice cream in my cart. He knew the truth. So instead, I simply smiled and nodded, and did an impromptu little advertisement for Ben & Jerry's ice cream to amuse the kid. Good training food, I told him.

I think I silently wished him spinach for dinner, too.

Even later that same day, I had my annual checkup visit to the gynecologist's office. The doctor came in and instructed me to put my legs in a compromising position.

"Hey," he said suddenly, "aren't you a mountain climber?"

I sat up almost violently.

"Do you like spinach?" I demanded.

He let out a light, benevolent little laugh, as though the non sequitur made perfect sense.

It was the process of unpacking, two months after I returned home, of sifting through the duffel bags and separating Zee's things from my own, that provided the catharsis I needed.

I systematically went through each bag and each barrel in my storage shed, and removed everything that reminded me of our marriage.

I didn't try to stop myself from destroying the memories of Zee. It was a necessary ritual.

And then I discovered the hat inside an old boot. I looked at the hat for a stupefied moment before I stuffed it back in the boot.

It was the one remnant of Iñaki that had escaped Zee's destruction.

It was the same hat, still hidden in the old boot that I found when I was rummaging through my equipment a few months ago.

I HAD MEANT TO RETURN IT TO IÑAKI IN JANUARY 1997, when I went to Pamplona. It was a foolish journey, that trip.

It began as a journey to London. My grandfather had died at the beginning of December, at home.

I had traveled to England two years before to help him through a period when my grandmother was in the hospital. The night she went in for the surgery, the clock on the dining room mantel suddenly stopped ticking. My grandfather had been fixated on it, restlessly pacing back and forth between the sitting room and the dining room, pausing to gaze steadily at the hands of the clock over his spectacles. Somehow under the weight of his stare, it faltered and then stopped. I think his heart stopped ticking in that moment, too.

He probably would have willed it to stop for longer than a moment if he could have. The steady predictable presence of my grandmother was what kept him moving. The idea of life continuing without her terrified him.

He was spared his fears; the clock was resuscitated, and my grandmother survived the surgery. She was the one, two years later, who was left behind. And so my plan was to travel to England, to help see her through the period of grief after the holidays, after all the other adults in the family had returned home.

Iñaki and I both had ambitions to go to Kanchenjunga in the spring. We would be two out of fewer than 30 climbers on the mountain. It would be almost impossible to ignore each other's presence.

Meet me in London, I proposed.

Come to Pamplona, he suggested. You can train with our team for a week or two.

And so, while my aunt from Saudi Arabia took care of my grandmother, I flew from London to Madrid, and caught a train from Madrid to Pamplona.

THE FIRST DAY OF TRAINING IN NORTHERN SPAIN WAS A DAY of backcountry skiing. Oh, God, I thought, I didn't know we were going to go *skiing*.

Minor problem number one: I hadn't brought any hardware or serious snow gear with me, owing to the fact that I was AWOL from a trip to visit my grandmother.

Minor problem number two: I had never been skiing above tree line, in avalanche terrain, 20 kilometers from the nearest road. I grew up on the East Coast, skiing groomed trails on packed powder. There are no cliffs on these trails.

Problem number one was easy to solve. One of Iñaki's friends had an extra pair of skis and men's boots five sizes too large. I stuffed an extra pair of socks in the toes, figured out how the bindings worked, and reasoned (prayed) that they would probably snap off each time I fell.

Problem number two was unsolvable, so I decided to ignore it.

On the way to the trailhead, I leaned forward in the back seat of the car, straining to overhear snippets of the conversation between Iñaki and the driver in the front seat. They were laughing, punctuating the dialogue with hand and head gestures. Whack, a hand clapping and glancing off a forearm. Like a body hitting and glancing off a tree, I supposed.

Avalanchas...perritos. Cruzes... Madre de... golpes.

Avalanches. Little dogs. Crosses (did they mean traversing or the religious kind?). Mother of smacks and bruises.

I sat back and looked out the window.

There was a fresh foot of snow up in the mountains, on top of an already fat base. We trundled bodies and skis out of cars. I was wired with nervous energy.

The approach, it turned out, was long, a two- or three-hour contemplative rite of passage through a tunnel of snow-laden fir boughs.

As soon as I realized this, I pulled out to the front to share the work of breaking trail. Iñaki had seven men on his Kanchenjunga team. As the only woman, I knew I had to outperform the others, at least on the way up. This is immature but completely irrefutable. Show me a woman in the mountains who does not feel that she has to try to carry twice as much or do twice as much work as her male partners, and I'll show you a woman who is sharing her tent. To stabilize the gender dynamics, you have to be unavailable— either engaged with a member of the group or universally respected, out of reach.

We reached the top of the tree line. The winds had whipped snow from the back side of the mountain, forming an overhanging lip at the top, a cornice that cast shadows on the pillows and slabs of snow below. We climbed up the lee side of the ridge, and then there were five of us standing up on that little lip. Five of us, looking into a white abyss.

Not all skiers are created equal.

One of Iñaki's friends was a gravity dog. He jumped off the cornice, popped a roller, rode on an invisible swell of air that let him defy gravity for a few seconds before he found salvation with two skis planted firmly on Earth.

Another was a powder hound. He reveled in the opportunity to ski virgin snow, caressing the curves of the slope with his poles, carving ripples of passion with his skis, undulating hips and shoulders.

The third was a rhythm pup. He boogied down the hill, a loose goose dancing through the hollows and moguls and drops.

I watched him execute two deft turns and then launched my body over the edge, toes crimped tightly to control boot slippage.

I am a mongrel, I decided. A gravity-rhythm-powder pooch.

Like the gravity dog, I flew through space. Instead of landing on two skis, though, I landed on my face, like the powder hound. I left my signature on the hill, a kind of dot-to-dot line down the face of the slope. And like the rhythm pup, my body fell in a natural, predictable cadence. Pole plant, pole plant, catch an edge, face plant. The face plant was often followed by an exceptionally acrobatic, if not graceful, horizontal rolling pirouette.

One of those was marred by crossed skis, which produced a sharp knee twinge at the moment of impact. Awash in a bath of sweat, I leaned on my poles and observed the offending body part with a flash of irritation. It seemed to be able to hold weight in all directions, more or less. That was good; we still had to ski back to the road. A stretched ligament, I presumed. I can't remember the rest of the journey down, probably because some gland in my body cranked out a mother lode of chemicals to mask the pain.

"You are good at going up," Iñaki observed with a smile back at the car, "but not so good at coming down. You were that way on Gasherbrum, too, very fast going up and slow going down. That could be a problem on Kanchenjunga. You have to run away from the summit before the mountain realizes you are there."

I grimaced. I hated it when he made wise comments like that. Especially in simplified English, with that rich Euro-accent and the sincere smile.

We continued to train for a couple of days. When Iñaki recognized the limp in my gait, he refused to continue running. "There are limits. You are not listening to the pain or your intuition," he told me angrily. "You are obsessed."

"I am *not* obsessed," I retorted. He would call me hard instead of obsessed if I were male, I said to myself, seething. Why is enduring a little pain considered a sign of strength for a Ukrainian or Polish man, and a sign of neurosis for an American or British woman?

The next day, Iñaki lounged around the apartment, returning phone calls from sponsors and media. I borrowed his bicycle, still angry, and rode for five hours. It was a wasted day. Even with aspirin, I couldn't seem to move my knees fast enough to get my heart rate up into the aerobic zone. There were deeper issues, of course. During the months of absence, we had imagined each other dreaming of each other, as we ourselves were dreaming. Despite our pledge to remain just friends, we had cast invisible nets of expectations and familiarity around each other.

In our dreams, we had flown side by side; we had circled the globe in a synchronized flight. In our realities, when we touched our wings got tangled in those nets, and we fell to the Earth.

I HAD TO GO BACK TO LONDON AFTER THE FALL, OF COURSE.

I walked through the train station with Iñaki, wishing he'd let me purchase the tickets, wishing he'd leave and leave me alone. But he was trying to cauterize his own raw emotions, and so we collided and bungled even the good-byes.

The train station was a hollow, echoing hall, a collage of pillars and shades of light and darkness, a kaleidoscope of dissonant sounds and forms.

I was empty. Determined not to feel any pain.

I climbed onto the train, swung my bag up into an overhead rack, and then slumped into the seat empty-handed. No book. I knew I wouldn't be able to think or read.

I stared at my reflection in the window, my eyes floating small and black in sunken cheeks bathed in a fluorescent pall. Loneliness and sadness took turns clutching at my throat. I breathed carefully, in, out, in, out, measuring the breaths. No tears. You can drown in tears.

Lights blipped past in the darkness beyond the glass. An hour passed, and then two. My eyes continued to stare, unblinking. They were rimmed with redness. I tried to conjure up an image of Iñaki in the blank blackness of the window, thinking I could then slowly, carefully, begin to deliberately erase him, bit by bit. But I couldn't see him. I couldn't seem to remember anything about him, the shape of his hands or the expression in his eyes.

After a while, I couldn't even see my own reflection. I was looking into another abyss, this one dark instead of blinding white.

Humankind has not woven the web of life.
We are but one thread in it.
Whatever we do to the web, we do to ourselves.
All things are bound together.
All things connect.

— CHIEF SEATTLE

MAIN STREET

"**Y**ou're not falling asleep, are you?" Hiddle suddenly asked.

"No," I adjusted my posture defensively.

Just then the cupped ears of a frightened deer appeared in the periphery of my vision. He was standing rigidly in the middle of the highway, frozen with fear in my headlights. I made an unsuccessful attempt to swerve without spinning into the next lane, and then felt a thump that reverberated through my own body as the front end of the car hit him square in the rump.

In the rearview mirror I could see him leaping across the wide band of snow at the edge of the highway, a ball of pain streaking through the night.

"We'd better stop for coffee," I said.

Hiddle nodded. We were both unnerved by the deer. "The next exit's where I get off," he remarked.

I glanced at him quickly. Did he really mean that? Dropping him off so suddenly somehow seemed improbable.

"Do you want me to take me wherever you're going?" I asked. "I've got some time. I don't mind going off the highway."

He shook his head, "No, I'll wait until eight o'clock or so and then give my friend a call. It's too early to arrive now."

And so, at the next exit, Hiddle hopped out of the car as suddenly and as simply as he had gotten in it.

I grabbed a cup of coffee at a drive-thru and then got back on the highway. It was only another hour or so home.

IT WAS ALMOST 6:00 A.M. WHEN I DROVE INTO TOWN, SO I went to the bagel shop first. The snow had stopped, finally, and the streets were a quiet, sloppy mess in the dim gray light of the morning.

I stood in line at the bagel shop, a disheveled wreck in the fleece sweater I had been wearing for 24 hours, caffeine percolating out of my pores and black shadowy circles under my eyes. Ahead of me was a tall man in a long wool trench coat. He had that morning's *Wall Street Journal* tucked neatly under his left arm, and a navy blue cashmere scarf wrapped carefully around his neck. I wondered what it would be like to come home after a day at an office in Manhattan and snuggle up with a wife in a big bed under a 300-weight goose down duvet. A regular man, I thought with a twinge of envy. He ordered black coffee and a bran muffin. Yes, a very regular man.

I ordered a raisin bagel with vegetable cream cheese to quell the little spasms of nausea in my stomach, plus another milky cup of coffee to counter the drowsy effect of the bagel, and retreated to my car to meditate and eat.

I slouched down in the driver's seat, immediately felt an over-powering need to sleep, and quickly sat up, thinking I'd better open the car door and go for a walk to jolt my senses awake. I had been driving all night, through a snowstorm, to be home to put Devi on the school bus at 8:55.

A path had been shoveled from the street to the sidewalk, but the neatness, the squareness of the edges offended me. Walk on this little strip of safety and you won't get snow on your shoes. Step right here and you won't slip. I stepped in the middle of the snow bank instead.

I dawdled on the sidewalk, unable to decide which way to turn. I was too tired. The ability to make simple decisions is one of the first mental capacities to be diminished by fatigue. I learned this as a graduate student, when I smacked my head on a lamppost after an all-night study session. I saw the post coming, knew I was on a path that would intersect with a solid object. I just couldn't decide which way to turn.

So I simply stood outside the Horologist of London's shop, nursing a cup of coffee and blowing on my cold, chapped fingers. In the window was a beautiful mantel clock rimmed with golden roses in the window, hands frozen in place. Five fifty-five, the clock said. Facing it, a towering imperial grandfather. 8:22. Next to that, a cherry-wood tall case, frozen at 6:24.

Grunsell Associates, the sign read. On the door was a placard: By appointment on Mondays, Tuesdays, and Wednesdays. Which one of all those clocks, I wondered, do Mr. Grunsell and his associates use to keep appointments?

I pressed my face closer to the window, peering inside to see if there was a timer filled with sand. On the beach as a child I liked to fill my hands with fine, dry sand, the kind you would find up near the dunes, and let it run through my fingers. It was a race, then, to see which hand or which finger gap would drain first. Now it would be a competition to see which could hold on to the sand the longest. Or maybe simply a challenge to let the grains flow through each hole at a measured pace, at exactly the same rate. Parallel realities, parallel strands of time, streaming like ribbons into the sand at my feet.

A gust of wind rattled the crispy brown leaves in the oak overhead. It was cold. I hunched my shoulders up, took another sip of the coffee, and burrowed my chin and mouth down into the collar of my fleece.

It is always difficult, this process of returning to civilization after an expedition. Everything is very comforting and at the same time vaguely bewildering.

Next to the horologist, a new shop. Touch of Sedona: Southwest Gifts & Healing Center. I gazed up at the white lights strung up in the tree outside, a field of little artificial winking eyes of fate. There was a row of dream catchers hanging in the window. Concentric circular spider webs. Sieves to hang over the cradles of Native American babies to filter out bad dreams.

"Whatever we do to the web," Chief Seattle said, "we do to ourselves."

At the center of each circle there was nothing. A hole. I read somewhere that the Ojibwa clans traditionally put a feather in that hole in the center of the dream catcher; it meant breath, or air. It fluttered, and taught infants about breathing, and the importance of good air, and the flowing movements of the spirit.

Are there dream catchers for our adult dreams and ambitions, I wondered, to sift out the bad ones out and let the good ones slip through?

PART TWO

1999 – 2000

*No one remembers who climbed Everest the
second time.*

— Na Nook

EVEREST: ELEPHANT IN A DARK HOUSE

After we returned from K2 in the fall of 1998, I wanted to go back. That much I knew. But how, and with whom, and when?

Slowly, over the winter, between conferences, festivals, and trips all over North America to climb and give slide show presentations, a plan emerged. Chris was interested in returning to K2, and he might be available to help with some of the logistics and planning.

Iñaki was also interested. National Geographic TV was looking for a cameraman to film the expedition. He traveled to Washington in February 1999 to meet with them and accepted their offer. We had climbed together peacefully on Kanchenjunga in 1997. I figured we could do it again.

Phoning, faxing, and e-mailing across a span of six thousand miles, we pieced together an outrageously bold plan. Instead of "just" going to K2, we would acclimatize first on Everest, climbing as high as possible in a lightweight style, without the aid of supplemental oxygen or high-altitude Sherpas. Our goal on Everest was to reach at least 26,000 feet (8,000 meters), beef up our red-blood-cell counts, and hone our ability to work together as a team. Then we would, if all went well, attempt an alpine-style ascent of K2.

Much of the funding for the project was provided by the National Geographic Society Expeditions Council. NATIONAL GEOGRAPHIC magazine issued a writer's contract for the K2 attempt, and they promised to find a photographer for K2 while we were on Everest. For Everest we found a climber-photographer named Bobby Model.

Everything pulled together so rapidly and so smoothly that I felt like I was riding a huge swell in a rapidly coursing river. I half expected to wake up one morning and see a whirlpool, an enormous eddy just around the bend. And that's just what happened on Everest.

THE TIBETANS CALL IT CHOMOLUNGMA. THE NEPALESE called it Sagamartha. The original surveyors considered these and other names—Devadhunka, Chingopamari—and finally settled on Mount Everest. Despite the surveyors' official declaration, it is still a mountain of many names. After a slide show about Himalayan climbing to raise money, an astute six-year-old kid came up to me with a look of pure enlightenment on his face. "Now I know why they call it Everest," he announced, "Because you never get to rest!"

Mount Neverest?

Whatever you choose to call it, the point on the globe designated by the coordinates 27° 57' N and 86° 56' E is unquestionably the highest point on Earth. This distinction is both a blessing and a curse. For cultures that value superlatives, Everest has become a suitable hook to hang dreams on. For cultures that value harmony, Everest has become an outcast—a mountain defiled, stripped of its real meaning.

In 1922, the chief lama of the Rongbuk Monastery called the members of the British Everest expedition heretics. "I was feeling very sick," he wrote about the proposed meeting with George Mallory and his group. Nonetheless, he gave them gifts of meat and tea and warned them, "As our country is bitterly cold and frosty, it is difficult for others than those who are devoted to religion not to come to harm. As the local spirits are furies, you must act with great firmness."

Places can change people.

Seventy-five years later, after the Everest tragedy of 1996, Jon Krakauer cited a Sherpa who posted a message on an Internet bulletin board: "I have never gone back to my homeland because I feel it is cursed. My ancestors arrived in the Solo-Khumbu region fleeing from persecution in the lowlands. There they found sanctuary in the shadow of 'Sagarmathaji,' 'mother goddess of the earth.' In return they were expected to protect that goddesses' sanctuary from outsiders. But my people went the other way. They helped outsiders find their way into the sanctuary and violate every limb of her body by standing on top of her, crowing in victory, and dirtying and polluting her bosom.... I have vowed never to return home and be part of that sacrilege."

I wasn't ignoring these concerns in going to Everest. In fact, it was part of my quest. Surely, I thought, there must be a way to climb on the mountain in a peaceful manner. Surely what matters is the way in which climbers climb, not our mere presence. Surely there is a way to show respect for the soul of the mountain.

THE JOURNAL I KEPT ON EVEREST IS CHOPPY, DISCONSOLATE. It gives little glimpses of the ways in which the landscapes without and within us shifted and interacted and changed. "Sunset in Pheriche is a sight I will never forget," I wrote on the third day of our approach, "Viscous amber clouds piled up the flanks of Ama Dablam and other peaks, churning and frothing, tumbling over each other in some desperate, operatic quest for space. It is strange how the mountains limit the clouds. Earlier today we went up the valley to Dingboche. It was supposed to be just a quick jaunt, scoping the terrain to shoot some footage, but we all got a little carried away by some impulse to push higher, and higher, and wound up just climbing for most of the day. I think Bobby started it. He suggested an excellent and innovative means of acclimatization, a competition to see how far we could each run up hill while holding our breath. Up and up, gasping and running past each other. We ran up into the clouds, and even after the others had stopped running, I couldn't stop. I didn't stop until I ran out of rungs and stairs in the clouds, at the top of a rocky peak called Pokalde, some 2,000 feet higher than Everest Base Camp."

Only four of us took that little jaunt—Chris, Bobby, our producer David, and I. Two days earlier, in Tengboche, Iñaki had left our team. It was a bizarre, sudden decision. I had woken up to the tinkling of yak bells and the instant awareness that something was wrong. I rubbed my eyes and stumbled out of the lodge to find water.

Outside, Iñaki was talking with David. It was a sight I will never forget. In stark contrast to the two of them, in their matching burgundy fleece jackets, was a group of Tibetan Buddhist monks, in matching burgundy robes, huddled on the steps of the Tyangboche monastery. Iñaki was shouting angrily, the monks were quietly watching. All against the background of the vibrant lush green of the meadow and the white swirling uncertainty of the mists and clouds.

I knew better than to interrupt. Later, we would all try to decipher the meaning of that morning. Iñaki, it turned out, was refusing to continue. David was willing to make any concession, but Iñaki was refusing to accept any offer. He would, he said defiantly, continue up to Base Camp on his own, and climb without the camera.

I racked my brain for something our group might have done or said to offend him, some unintentional blunder, and couldn't come up with anything significant.

It didn't make sense. From my point of view his actions seemed incomprehensibly unprofessional and selfish. He was jeopardizing the entire project.

By the time we reached Base Camp, I realized that our group wasn't the only one exhibiting odd behavior. "We're at Everest Base Camp now," I wrote in my journal in April 1999, "and despite a very cushy trek with latrines, meals, and mattresses along the way, both Chris and I are already longing for the rugged loneliness of K2. Traveling en masse with hundreds of trekkers and dozens of climbers is a new experience, one that I'm not sure I'd care to repeat."

It was not simply that there were swarms of people. In fact, that particular season saw a pronounced dip in the number of climbers on the south side. It was more that a different atmosphere prevailed, a different spirit emerged from the amazing kaleidoscope of climbers and styles and goals.

In any given year, there is a colorful patchwork of individual climbers who are out for firsts on the mountain of superlatives. The 1999 contenders included the youngest (a 15-year-old boy), the first Swedish woman, the first climber to spend the night on the summit, the first climber with exercise-induced asthma, and the first cowboy to wave a Wyoming flag and twirl a lasso at 29,000 feet. Each of these climbers brought unique and in some cases widely divergent motivations to the mountain, with correspondingly divergent styles. Some climbed with oxygen, some without. Some tagged on to a private permit, others acted as an independent unit within a guided or commercial group, others were guided clients, and still others found work as guides to finance the ambition.

The "est" factor, as I like to call it, is what attracts westerners to Everest. The biggest, tallest, bestest. Some of them go there hoping the "est" will rub off on them. They want to become the highest, the fastest, the firstest.

Of course, some climbers simply want to test their limits. And many of the significant achievements on Everest (fortunately) go unreported by the media. The headline story "Couple Breaks High-Altitude Sex Barrier," for example, has never been leaked to the press.

I was aching during the trek, and for most of the climb, trying to understand what had happened that morning in Tyangboche, why Iñaki had left the expedition. Several days after we arrived at Base Camp, my journal shows the first signs of comprehension.

"Spoke to Iñaki today," I wrote tersely. "He said Pete and Andy made it through the Ice Fall in two and a half hours on their first trip, and that he made it in an hour and 24 minutes, without really pushing. Really, was all I could think of to say to this remarkable achievement. I am bewildered, I don't even know how to communicate with him any more. On GII, on Kanchenjunga, he would have come down off the mountain with a joke or a comment about the air or the snow. Not this obscene bravado."

On GII and Kanchenjunga, Iñaki was a different climber.

So was I. The two of us fought continuously, childishly, on Everest. I was bitter, confused. I was only just beginning to understand that mountains can shape people.

EVEREST IS LIKE THE ELEPHANT IN THE SUFI PARABLE OF THE Elephant in a Dark House. The parable was originally told by Rumi, a thirteenth century Islamic mystic, who found divine inspiration for his stories while spinning around a pillar.

"There was an elephant in a dark house," he related one day, whirling in a meditative trance, "Many people went to see it and had to enter the dark stable to do so. Because it was so dark they could not make out the form of the elephant at all and had to work with their hands to identify its being, each person using his palm to find the shape. The hand of one fell on the creature's trunk and he said, 'This is a water pipe.' The hand of another touched the ear and found a fan. Another handled the elephant's leg and found a pillar, while another touched the back and discovered a throne. There were those who heard descriptions from these folk and made their own identifications, and there were still others who interpreted one shape as against another, all very diverse and contrary."

Everest is like Rumi's elephant. Every climber touches some part of a beast we cannot name, and feels something different. Some feel pride and valor. Some feel the pull of fate. Caressing the folds of the elephant's skin, my own hands felt the by then familiar form of the labyrinth, that twisted network of passages and turns, the maze of opportunities and options and dead ends.

What Rumi didn't say, perhaps what he deliberately omitted, was that hands and the objects they caress become one. My hands have become a labyrinth. The lines and crevices have deepened. There is a twisted maze—history and future, chance and choices— etched into them.

"YOU DON'T TRUST ME," IÑAKI SAID JUST BEFORE HE LEFT Everest Base Camp. The accusation was tinged with a mocking kind of sadness. We had both gotten high on the mountain but neither of us had made the summit.

"Trust doesn't have anything to do with this problem," I retorted. "The problem is you've morphed into someone I can't even communicate with."

I felt deserted, betrayed. Without him, the expedition had ended before it even started. True, Chris and I could still climb together. But with the added task of filming and carrying all of the cameras and other equipment for filming and photography, our already ambitious project became even more ambitious. There was also the problem of finding a cameraman we knew and could trust for K2. Finding a climber with solid filming experience who would be as strong as Iñaki at high altitudes, we all realized, would be impossible.

"You know, Heidi," David said when we reached base Camp, "if you want to throw in the towel now, nobody is going to blame you. We'll all support your decision, and we can look for another cameraman for next year."

But we didn't quit on Everest. In fact, we accomplished our original goal to acclimatize for K2, climbing in "lightweight" style, without supplemental oxygen. We were even planning to continue on to K2. In the third week of May, our editor at NATIONAL GEOGRAPHIC magazine sent an e-mail to Base Camp. The photographer they had chosen for K2 had gone to 17,000 feet without acclimatization on a trip to South America and was still recovering from HAPE (High Altitude Pulmonary Edema). His doctor wouldn't clear him for the K2 expedition. The editorial staff would understand if we wanted to continue, the e-mail explained, but they would prefer if we postponed the expedition. Reading that e-mail, we all agreed that the wisest thing to do would be to go home and reorganize the expedition for 2000.

We boil at different degrees.

— RALPH WALDO EMERSON

WARNING SIGNS

I should have stayed home. I should never have gone back to K2, at least not with the "K2 OOO" team. I know that now, and I knew it then.

There were so many warning signs.

There was the National Geographic Society Expeditions Council's hesitation and withdrawal of financial support.

There were the endless hours on the phone with the expedition leader, Jeff Alzner, trying to walk him through the logistics of procuring sponsorship. Endless hours of dealing with his impatient tirades.

Then there was the trip to Oregon the weekend before the expedition, to Jeff's house, where Jeff and two of the other team members, Paul and Gill, were frantically packing more than three tons of equipment.

Trying to organize an expedition the north side of K2 amidst the chaos of a full-scale remodeling project, Jeff had boxes and barrels and equipment strewn everywhere. Somehow, in the process of restructuring his entire house, running his horticultural business, and leading an 18-member expedition, he had neglected the basics. There were no utensils in the kitchen to cook with; he went to restaurants for meals. There was no shower curtain in the bathroom; I'm not sure what he did about that. The sheer magnitude of the stress and chaos should have tipped me off to the obvious. Jeff is not good at delegating. "A control freak," one of the journalists covering the expedition called him.

I had serious last-minute reservations about climbing with Paul and Gill, too. The tension between Jeff and Paul and Gill during those two days was thicker than the dust on the kitchen counters.

"Paul? Where the hell are those guys?" Jeff muttered grimly as we walked into the house. "They're supposed to be here. They were supposed to do the food shopping this morning. I told Gill to make a list. Now I have to do all the goddamn *shopping*, too." His eyes were bulging with rage, and the fist not holding his cell phone was balled up as he stalked back and forth between the couch and his desk, trying to figure out who to call to track down Paul and Gill.

The arguing had been so loud and so crude, I was told quietly by one of the cameramen there to film the packing process, that the film crew the day before doing interviews with the team members had had to ask Paul and his girlfriend to leave. They had been hurling invectives at each other out in the driveway, and the audio guy two floors up couldn't block out the background noise.

I had met Paul and Gill nine months before, at a general expedition meeting at Jeff's house. I knew even then that we wouldn't be the best of pals. But of course with a group of 12 climbers, I knew I'd get along with some, and some I wouldn't. Still, I didn't anticipate anything this extreme.

Later that night, Gill was missing again. It was 1:30. The bars were closed. Paul and his girlfriend went out to search for him.

"F—ing Gill," Jeff told me when I asked the next morning, teeth clenched, "passed out on the goddamn floor of the joint. These guys are supposed to be here helping me, and instead I'm their goddamn baby-sitter!" Gill, it turned out, had gone to some joint to nurse his anger over a recent divorce.

"I'd stay away from him," one of Jeff's friends advised. "He's not too psyched about humans of the female kind."

AS I SAID, I SHOULD HAVE STAYED AT HOME.

Don't ask me why I went.

I thought I could handle them.

It was only five days before we were scheduled to leave. Maybe I was concerned about promises and commitments, obligations to sponsors.

Or perhaps it was just that familiar allure of K2, that irresistible tugging, the restless night dreams.

To be fair to the climbers who were on the K2000 Expedition, I should warn readers that I am still experiencing a sort of emotional block in sorting through the aftermath and meaning of the craziness of the expedition.

The experiences described in the first part of this book occurred more than two years ago. I have been home from the north side of

K2 for only three months. My narration in this section is a reflex, an instinctive and immediate response to an equally aberrant series of events.

The term "emotional block" itself requires some explanation. In 1998, roughly at the same time that we were climbing on the south side of K2, an American named Ben Lecomte was testing his limits by swimming across the Atlantic Ocean. According to an online British newspaper, the *Electronic Telegraph*, Lecomte experienced a temporary "emotional block" in the middle of his swim, when he decided to take a 500-mile detour after he was pursued by a great white shark who swam 30 feet below him for several days.

I suppose the primal terror that floods your mind when you confront a shark or an avalanche or a gaping crevasse *could* be described as an emotional block. It's not exactly the kind of problem that could easily be tweaked by sitting on a psychologist's couch, though, and certainly not the kind of emotional block I am feeling in relation to the events on the north side of K2.

There *is* that sort of brain freeze that sometimes sets in when you're dangling off a very thin 7mm rope, 23,000 feet up on K2 and 4,000 feet above a glacier. You look up at the rope stretching over a sharp lip of granite, and suddenly something akin to reason flickers across your oxygen-impoverished brain, and you suffer the realization that if the rope breaks at that particular moment, you will accelerate to 180 miles per hour and then, after 15 long seconds to pray, decelerate to zero miles per hour. Contemplating those 15 seconds can send the mind down a twisted path that ultimately leads to either a suburban life or spiritual enlightenment. But I don't think I'd describe this as an emotional block, either.

No, the emotional block that I am experiencing in writing about the K2 O O O Expedition doesn't have anything to do with risk or staring into the depths of the soul on a solo experience. It stems from the kind of heart-wrenching desires that interfere with your ability to intuit the vagaries of the mountain and the forces around you. Emotions so strong that they block your ability to maintain a healthy interpersonal relationship with your climbing partners. A festering anger, the kind that would lead you to wish someone something much worse than spinach for dinner, falls into this category.

Anyone who has been confined to a tent with a couple of gnarly climbers in a storm with avalanches and high winds and other mildly annoying objective hazards compounding the misery will appreciate this sage piece of advice: choose your partners carefully. Because 99 of every 100 high-altitude climbers are male, this nugget of wisdom is especially important if you happen to be a woman. Certainly when you find yourself in a tent or a portaledge smaller than the size of a twin bed for days on end.

I have climbed exclusively with men, primarily because there are so few women currently climbing 8,000-meter peaks. There have been only a handful of women on either side of K2 in the past five years.

Some male climbers think that being the only female climber in a base camp of 100 or so men is an enviable position.

They're right. It is.

You see, women enjoy some distinct and completely unfair advantages. On one expedition I was able to procure an entire half-barrel of chocolate bars in exchange for an outdated issue of *Playboy*,

and I'm fairly certain that I wouldn't have been as successful in nego-
tiating such an astronomical exchange rate if I had been male. On
another expedition I was introduced to a British climbing celebrity
who has the largest male appendage in the Himalaya. I know,
because he told me.

Of course there are also some disadvantages. When you are the
only female climber in a base camp of between 25 and 200 men,
your partners tend to arouse a bizarre emotion sometimes described
as "jealousy" in other men, and the miserable situations often get
blown out of proportion, no matter how hard you try to remain
aloof. On Kanchenjunga, one particularly vocal Italian climber from
another team asked a liaison officer who didn't speak English to
sign a letter to the Ministry of Tourism claiming that I was
climbing on the wrong route. My mere presence as a female on the
mountain, he announced to anyone who would listen, was "ruin-
ing the group psychology" of his expedition. The group psychology?
It was the first time I had ever heard this term used in the context
of Himalayan climbing.

I am not the only woman who has experienced difficulties in
maintaining healthy relationships as the only female member of a
climbing team.

Wanda Rutkiewicz, for example, commented on the importance
of having a "guardian angel" on an expedition. "For a woman to
be accepted," she said, "she has to outdo men, and free herself from
the old stereotypes. Men are happy to have a woman along provided that she is charming, cheerful, a nice little mascot with no
great sporting ambitions. They are usually feeling a little homesick,
and she can serve as a house-mother substitute. But put an inde-

pendent woman into an expedition without a guardian angel—that is, a husband or a male friend—and let her claim acceptance on terms of equality and without exploiting her femininity; the result will probably be conflict or even the failure of a whole project."

If I had had a guardian angel on the K2000 expedition, things would have been significantly easier.

Over the years, I have climbed with a diverse range of partners, with correspondingly diverse interests, idiosyncrasies, and tent behavior.

Ego Man was very good at counting, especially in the tent. He counted the number of peaks he had climbed, the number of pitches he had led, the number of pounds he had carried, the number of times he had had to melt snow. Conversations with Ego Man were simple, even elegant. "You took up 68 percent of the volume and consumed 75 percent of the oxygen in the tent last night," he would say.

"Did not."

"Did too."

Gear Man knew the brand name and weight of every item of equipment in the tent. We spent many excited hours talking about a new idea for improving the curve-aspect-pick-shaft-ratio of a 50cm third tool.

Hard Man ate horse fat with mustard and wore his left boot a size smaller after losing three toes, probably while attempting to solo Everest naked.

Lonely Man sighed and shivered a lot.

Crazy Man complained about the wife who took care of his daughter at home and was demented enough to think being married to a female climber would be better.

Absent-minded Professor Man forgot his pee bottle, wanted to share mine, and then very generously offered to let me borrow his toothbrush in exchange. Conversations with him were generally about topics like possible model theoretic constructs for the mathematical relationship between discrete and continuous infinities.

Joke Man always carried white chocolate and had a five-hour repertoire of jokes about sheep and shipwrecked men and poodles.

On the K2OOO Expedition, none of these particular personalities were present.

There were Jeff and Paul and Gill. Jeff described himself as "headstrong." I am tired of arguing with him, so I won't dispute this one. Add Headstrong Man to the list above. Both Paul and Gill, climbers and friends from California, have a voracious appetite for clear beverages. Paul prefers tequila, Gill prefers mescaline. Tequila Man and Mescal Man, although they deserve other, much more colorful titles. Then there was Shawn, a climber from Alaska. Shawn described himself, in a website dispatch, as "selfish." I think this is going too far; he is not truly selfish, just self-absorbed and self-centered. Self Man captures all versions. And there was Mike, a seasoned climber from Colorado. One of the journalists traveling with our group described Mike as "Mr. Nice Guy." Yet Mike described Jeff as the "Little Tyrant," and me as a "Tonya Harding."

And so on.

There were two other women in our group of 18 at Base Camp, but neither of them were climbing on the mountain, and both were involved with men on the team. Both had what Wanda would have called a guardian angel.

Add to these personalities the fact that there were 29 days of snow in July, in which we were all stuck at Base Camp together.

Throw in the fact that only six of the thirteen members of the climbing team had any prior experience on an 8,000-meter peak. The other seven were on their first Himalayan climbing expedition. At least four of those had never climbed outside of the U.S.

And, for good measure, add the pressures of making a documentary film and journalists reporting live from Base Camp for two websites and a newspaper.

It was a recipe for a miserable experience.

Yes, I should have known better.

MISHAPS

The team began to fall apart even before we got out of the airport in New York City. There was a string of mishaps, some predictable, some not.

The first was the delayed flight and missing baggage problem. With a total of 152 bags, 36 of them being transported as personal baggage by 16 team members flying into New York on 4 different airlines, little glitches in the baggage transport system were to be expected. I could have predicted one or two missing bags, but not nine. One or two delayed arrivals, not 14.

The agent of chaos was a massive thunderstorm system that descended on the U.S. on the night before our departure. Six of the 16 members of the group flying to New York had to camp out in the Detroit and Denver airports. Four of those members arrived without their personal baggage.

Normally, missing baggage simply means buying a toothbrush

and relaxing while the airline tracks down the renegade articles and delivers them to the door of your destination. No big deal. In this particular case, however, we were all boarding a PIA flight to Islamabad. There would be no reasonable way to retrieve the bags once we left the country. And what we needed from the bags weren't toothbrushes, but crampons and ice axes and 8,000-meter down suits. Such specialized equipment would be impossible to obtain in Pakistan or China. It would be difficult to procure in the U.S., even given a week to make phone calls.

We crammed six people into the cabs of two trucks, and started driving back and forth between the airline offices and baggage claim areas at the JFK and LaGuardia airports in New York City.

Driving a truck in New York City is not easy under the best of circumstances. Commercial vehicles are not allowed on many of the parkways, and we didn't have a map. Four of the six of us also hadn't slept in at least 36 hours.

At one point we found ourselves approaching a stone arch bridge at 65 miles per hour. The middle of the arch was marked with a huge warning sign. Eight feet eight inches high. I winced. According to the rental agent at the truck company, the truck was ten feet seven inches high. I think I even ducked. After we went under the bridge, it took a few moments for my fogged, sleep-deprived brain to register the miraculous fact that the truck was not two feet shorter.

The driver, my friend Bill, was also looking as though he had just swerved to avoid an apparition of the Virgin Mary.

"Didn't we just violate the laws of physics?" I mumbled.

"I don't think so," he answered. "I accelerated to the speed of light, and veered out to the middle of the arch just before we passed through."

"*Mmm*," I nodded as though this made perfect sense. It did make perfect sense, at the time.

We clearly weren't going to be able to find the baggage that night, so 11 members of the team boarded the plane, and Pakistani International Airlines rebooked the remaining members on a flight two days later. Fortunately, the missing bags turned up on the day before the rescheduled flight.

This was followed by the cigarette mishap. Two members of the team who left on the originally scheduled flight were carrying 22 cartons of Camel cigarettes purchased in duty free as "incentive pay" for the camel drivers. In the mass exodus off the plane in Islamabad, after a 16-hour flight, the precious bag of smokes was somehow left in one of the overhead bins.

Panicked, Jeff called me from Islamabad. "We need Camels," he shouted into the phone.

I recognized the by then familiar agitation in his voice. "Don't worry, we'll have enough camels," I responded wearily, assuming he was talking for the umpteenth time about the number of camels we would need to transport our loads on the approach to the mountain, "We've done the math, it'll work out. Don't worry."

"No, not camels. *Camels!*" came the screaming response. "Cigarettes. I need you to buy 17 cartons of Camel straights. Got that?"

I had never bought a cigarette in my life. I had no idea what a Camel straight was.

"If I can't find Camel straights, are Camel bents O.K.?"

"No!" came the exasperated voice on the other end of the line. "Camel *straights*. Straight means they don't have filters. And don't wait to get them duty free at the airport, because they may not have them. We bought them all the other day."

"O.K.," I responded, wondering how and where I would get my hands on that many unfiltered cigarettes, and why cigarettes were the necessary sort of "incentive pay." I had never brought cigarettes on an expedition before. We were scheduled to return to the airport the following day. I was still trying to write dozens of thank-you notes to sponsors. The usual litany of last-minute details had popped up.

Bill agreed to go on a cigarette hunt. He came back four hours later. "There wasn't a single store in this entire area that stocked more than four cartons of Camel straights," he reported. "I had to go to six different places. One woman asked me why I needed so many cartons of Camels, why another cigarette wouldn't do. I tried to explain it had to be Camels because it was for a bunch of camel drivers in China, but I don't think she believed me."

PROBABLY THE MOST CRITICAL MISHAP, THE ONE THAT WAS to have the most far-reaching effects on the expedition, was losing the satellite telephone. It is not the kind of thing you can pick up at a corner store in Islamabad, and the particular unit our website sponsor had given us was not just any old sat phone. It was a $15,000 NERA M4 World Communicator Modem Unit, a high-data-rate phone that the technical trainer from the website had warned us was worth far more than a "measly 15K."

"There are only about 50 of these in the world," he explained, "and there's a waiting list to get one. The Queen of England wanted this one, but we managed to get it."

Aside from being a rare, expensive technological gem, the M4 phone and the transmissions of news and photos from the mountain were a vital part of the promises we had made to our sponsors. The $250,000 cost of the expedition had been largely offset by donations from contributors who expected to be able to contact us on site.

When and where did we lose it, you ask? On an x-ray machine belt in the JFK airport. How the hell did that happen? Jeff wanted to know, when I broke the news of the latest tale of woe to him in Islamabad.

Of the six of us boarding that second plane, three had slept less than ten hours in the previous five days. There were teary good-byes with family and friends just outside the x-ray area. There were at least five communal carry-on bags, and all of us were functioning at about 20 percent brain capacity. I was focused on tracking just the items of team equipment I was carrying, a laptop and a bundle of sponsorship dollars that had come in at the last minute. One of the other team members was responsible for the satellite phone, but I don't think he realized the value of what he was carrying.

Not until the layover in Manchester, England, did I think to double-check to make sure the Camels and all the other team necessities were on board. The satellite phone, I discovered, dumbfounded, wasn't. After a few moments of collective agonized memory searching, we traced it back to the x-ray machine in JFK.

Anyone could have picked it up.

The plane was about to take off. I begged a security officer who was doing a last-minute check of the plane to let me off, but he couldn't.

"Look," I said, wheels spinning frantically, "would you mind sending a fax? Here's the number. Just put the words 'urgent, sat phone, lost, dead meat, JFK, and x-ray' in the message. Dead meat should be in capital letters, please."

The guy actually sent a fax. He should go to heaven for that.

The fax was intercepted by Bill, who was savvy enough to decipher the desperate code, hop in the car, and speed two hours down to JFK airport. After a dozen or so calls, he managed to get through to the correct JFK security office on his cell phone on the way down. Could he give them a more specific description of the item than a "black bag?" they wanted to know. No, he said, but then he happened to remember that a "round compass-thingy with circles and lines" was in the outside pocket. Yes, they confirmed, that was enough to identify the item. A security officer had found it at the bottom of the metal ramp in the x-ray area and had brought it to a holding area.

Once Bill had retrieved the sat phone from security, we still had the problem of getting it to Islamabad on the first available flight. After it was received by the Islamabad Customs Agency, the satellite phone would have to go through a complex importation process instead of the normal airport customs, where you are typically simply waved past an airport security official in the arrivals area.

The clearance might be possible in one day, but it could take as much as three or four days. Our team was scheduled to depart from Islamabad in two days.

"Jeff," I said, "we need to wait for the sat phone. We can't leave without at least trying. We've got an obligation to sponsors, not just the website."

"Heidi," he said slowly, carefully, as though he were explaining something to a child, "this is a climbing expedition, not a phone expedition. We're here to climb a mountain, and I can't keep 18 people sitting around in Islamabad waiting for a goddamn phone!"

I shrugged. "You go, then. I'll stay." I'd be missing five critical days of time to "bond" with the team, I knew, but it seemed far more important to honor the obligations our team had to the people who had made the expedition possible.

So the group left on schedule, without me. "We're only going to wait one day for you at the border post in China," Jeff warned. "You'd better be there."

I remained in Islamabad with Greg Ritchie, one of the cameramen working for National Geographic TV. Greg stayed because he felt he had a duty to document this "angle" of the expedition.

Our first step was to contact Greg Mortensen, an American climber and former nurse who was working in Pakistan, running a nonprofit aid organization called the Central Asia Institute. In the process of establishing three women's vocational centers and 12 primary schools in Pakistan's Northwest Territories, he had learned how to import items ranging from diapers to books and toothpaste. Greg sent us his most trusted customs expert, Suleman Minhas.

Importing a piece of technology that is strictly forbidden, Suleman warned us in the car on the way to the Customs Agency, would be slightly more complex than importing diapers. Advanced technology is regarded with suspicion in Pakistan, particularly for travel in the Northwest Territories, where there are borders disputed with India and active military zones. Even with a pocket full of $600 (U.S.) in 100-rupee notes, he didn't know if it would be possible.

Anyone who wishes to import books or medicine or other items into Pakistan via legal means must possess the nerves of a bomb squad technician and the patience of Mother Teresa. You spend hour after hour moving from one officer to another, jostling other human beings in an anxious crowd clamoring for attention in a sweltering concrete airport hangar, wearing long sleeves and (if you are female) a *dopatta* to cover your head in 100-degree weather. You shout and wave papers until the object of your attentions, a customs officer, finally listens to your case.

Once he listens to your case, he will send you to another officer surrounded by another mob of waving hands and papers.

After four hours of shuffling back and forth and presenting the details of our request countless times, we were finally able to get the attention of a man sitting behind a desk labeled "Assistant Collector." Almost as soon as I mentioned the word "satellite phone," he produced an official-looking document detailing the permit procedure and other necessary paperwork required for satellite telephones. These typically take two months. Because we were climbing on the Chinese side of K2, and because we would be using the satellite phone only in China, we had not applied for a permit in Pakistan.

"Ah, but it says here *operable* satellite telephones." I handed the paper back to him, underlining the word with my finger. By this time I realized that I was going to have to resort to desperate measures to get the sat phone through. "My package is only a satellite telephone *part*. It is just an antenna, with some replacement parts. It is not *operable*, so it doesn't require a permit."

"A satellite part? Where is the rest of the phone?" the assistant collector asked, brow furrowed.

"With the rest of the team, on the way to China," I responded with what I hoped was a convincing and very innocent smile.

"Why have they left for China without you?" he asked.

"They are in a hurry to meet our Chinese customs agent at the border," I said. My mind raced for a means of proving that the team had actually already left, and suddenly remembered the Pakistani newspaper article from the previous day that the hotel receptionist happened to hand me on our way out the door that morning. "Look. Here," I pulled it out of my bag. "This article in the paper yesterday says that the team left Islamabad on Wednesday, May 24."

He scrutinized the article and then handed it back with a casual dismissive wave of his hand. "Go write the whole story down on paper and then come back," he instructed.

Suleman and I raced to find a stenographer's station with pen and paper, and I spewed out a slightly modified saga, a page of scrawling text in five minutes. When we returned, we discovered that Mr. Assistant Collector was at lunch. An agonizing half hour later, he was back and the paperwork was waved under his nose again. He silently wrote instructions to the customs security officers on the back of my application packet: "Inspect and catalog contents of package thoroughly. Package should contain only satellite antenna and replacement parts. Contents should in no way be operable. Record all model and serial numbers."

That posed a problem. You see, there is a handset for the phone that looks just like a cell phone. It is clearly not an antenna or replacement part, and with it, the unit is clearly operable. If the security officer inspecting the contents of the package saw the handset, I knew the game would be over. As we sweated and shuffled around the hangar, getting the appropriate forms and signatures for a security inspection, I was forming a desperate and demented but remotely possible plan. I was gambling that the handset was still in the outside pocket of the sat phone case. If it was in the outside pocket, with the azimuth chart and other accessories, perhaps he wouldn't see it right away. If I could somehow worm it out of the bag, while he was inspecting the antenna...maybe I could somehow slip it into the pocket of my baggy outfit...if I could somehow distract his attention....

Two hours, seven typewritten pages of paperwork and 15 little pink notes later, I finally found myself face-to-face with the security officer who had been called in to inspect the package. He pulled it out of the box very slowly, very carefully. I sat across from him, my hands folded politely in my lap. He opened the zipper of the main compartment and pulled out the antenna, very slowly, very carefully.

"What," he asked, peering with a wrinkled nose at the featureless gray hunk of metal, "is this?"

"I'm not sure, sir." I adjusted the dopatta wrapped around my head with a light shrug. "My technical man is with the team in China. I suppose it must be the antenna. Maybe it says something on the back."

He flipped the antenna open and squinted at the fine print on the back. "N-E-R-A World Communicator Antenna unit," he read, very slowly, enunciating every syllable.

Then he opened the outside pocket of the bag.

Suddenly there was a loud sound, like a gun, just outside the building. I pretended to be distracted by it. I held my breath and watched the security officer out of the corner of my eye. His hand pulled out a single transparent plastic bag full of sat phone accessories. The power cord. The dongle for connecting the PC card in the laptop. The extension cord. No handset.

It must still be in the bag, I reasoned, feeling the little twitch of a deviant smile tugging one corner of my mouth. I tried to breathe normally.

"Those must be the spare parts," I volunteered.

"How do you make a phone call?" he asked.

"I don't know, sir," I answered. I stood up to examine the phone with him, pulled the azimuth chart out of the outside pocket, and then set the bag down on the floor as though it were empty. The handset, I knew, was still inside. "There's some kind of a chart here," I continued, "but you would need something to dial numbers, right? The big box with the numbers on it must be in China. This is just the antenna and replacement parts."

"Hmm," he nodded, and very slowly, very carefully, he began recording every serial number of every part on the application package.

I handed each piece of equipment over, one by one, and then deftly repacked the bag for him when he was finished. I actually felt tentatively triumphant, but the process was nowhere near complete. We still had another two hours of paperwork to go.

Some time during those two hours, the Assistant Collector wrote a note in the back of my passport, very slowly, very carefully. "Pakistani Customs Islamabad AFO World Communicator Antenna Unit AFO S/No. QUFF911907RIACE0434, with adapter, power supply, and leads in case," he wrote, and signed his name at the bottom.

That's an awfully long serial number for something that is one of only 50 in the world, I thought to myself.

"You must show this passport and the antenna unit when you leave Islamabad in September," he instructed, "and you must show your passport and these papers at the border. We will call in advance to let them know you are coming."

What if the sat phone gets dropped in a river by a camel? Or stolen in China? I thought. Would that mean I'd be stuck in Pakistan indefinitely? Fortunately I'd thought to bring both my British and U.S. passports on the expedition.

And so, seven hours after our arrival and five minutes after the official closing time, I walked through the gates of the Islamabad Customs Agency with the NERA M4 phone safely in my hands.

Outside the gate, I found a slightly agitated Greg Ritchie. He had been waiting in the customs agent's office all day in the heat. "I tried to film you going into the compound this morning," he explained, "and I got arrested by the Islamabad police for filming in a restricted high-security area. I didn't know it was high security. It just looked like a normal street to me. I showed them the tape at the police headquarters to prove that it was just you that I was filming. They released me, but these guys in the customs agent's office wouldn't even let me out of the office for the rest of the day. They said I could get stoned for filming a woman."

"Hmm," I said, momentarily contemplating the what-ifs of the day. All in all, given the mishaps that could have happened, things had gone reasonably well.

WE HAD ONE LAST HURDLE BEFORE WE COULD FOLLOW THE planned itinerary of the expedition. We still had to catch up with the team. It was Thursday, May 25, 5:00 p.m. In order to reach Tashkurgan before the time at which Jeff had said they'd be leaving, on Saturday at noon, we would have to drive back to the hotel, grab our things, drive by truck or van overnight for 20 hours on the Karakoram Highway, somehow get through the Pakistani border control first thing in the morning Saturday, and then drive another six hours by jeep over the 15,500-foot high Khunjerab Pass to Tashkurgan.

The Karakoram Highway, as I had discovered on two previous expeditions, is not just any old highway. Greg Mortensen agreed to help us arrange a van and driver, but he was unhappy about the idea of our driving the worst stretches of the road at night.

"Going through Kohistan from Besham to Chilas at night," the note he had left at our hotel read, "is not advisable, especially between 1:00 and 3:00 a.m. Kohistan means 'land of the unforgivable' in Kohistani. If you have large sums of money, don't keep it in your main rucksack or on your body. If the local militia detains you, don't argue. They are very honest and they are bound by a tribal custom (Pattan) to guard you with their lives since you are their guest. Be careful."

When he appeared at the hotel with the van and driver, we asked for more details. In the previous year, he explained, there had been a number of incidents in Kohistan in which armed gangs had rolled large rocks out into the road as barricades and then hidden behind objects at the edge of the road. When the vehicle came to a stop, they had searched it for money and other valuables. If this happens, don't try to drive around or past the barricade, Greg advised; they will shoot at the back of the vehicle.

I nodded, thinking of the last time I had stopped in Chilas. The public bus I was riding had stopped there for lunch. A man near the wooden bench where I was eating was singing loudly, maniacally. His limbs were withered and waving wildly, and I assumed he was crippled. Some sort of cerebral palsy? I wondered. Curious, I had asked the shopkeeper who was serving lunch. The singing man's name was Sheikh, and he was crazy, the shopkeeper explained. He had killed his mother. Why? I wanted to know. Because his friends told him it would demonstrate courageousness and devotion to a cause. Then the man's friends deserted him, he explained. So now he is crazy. The shopkeeper had shrugged and smiled.

I thought about the comment in Greg's note, that the local militia was bound by a strong Pattan tribal custom to guard their guests with their lives. Pakistan is like that. It has traditionally been a crossroad for travelers, and most Pakistanis seem to have a very strong sense of duty as a host. Many regions are also very territorial. The villages in the Shegar Valley leading up to the Baltoro Glacier, for example, do not like to allow guides from southern Pakistan to work in their area.

In addition to the driver, Greg was sending a companion, Apo Abdul Razaq, with us. "Apo" means grandfather in Urdu. We asked him about his family, and he went through the fingers of about eight hands counting everyone: the total tally, I think, was three wives, twenty-three children, approximately three dozen grandchildren, and a smattering of great-grandchildren. The last of his own children was only three years old, which means there must be some extremely interesting family tree relationships. When we asked him how old he was, he produced his national identity card. According to the card, he was 56. Not possible, I objected. He grinned, and explained that after his second wife died, he didn't want to be any older than his third wife, so he had reported a different date of birth to the government.

The tally of the expeditions Apo Razaq has guided was no less amazing. Beginning with the second American K2 expedition in 1953, he rattled off a litany of climbers ranging from Charles Houston and Chris Bonington to Reinhold Messner and Doug Scott. He is still working as a guide, leading expeditions up the Baltoro, nurturing and feeding vagabond climbers from around the world dried apricots and biscuits.

At 1:00 a.m., after six hours on the road, the poor driver was clearly falling asleep at the wheel. I was up front, attempting to keep him going with the mere force of my presence. He pulled into a rest stop. The headlights of the van revealed several bodies in brown kurtas and pajamas lying outside on thatched cots. For a moment I wondered if they were corpses. Then one flopped an arm over the edge of a cot and rolled over in a restless dream.

I shot the driver an apprehensive glance. We can't stop, not now, I thought. This is Besham, the beginning of the danger zone Greg warned us about.

"You want to drive?" he asked me suddenly.

Drive? Me? A woman, wearing a shalwar kameez and a dopatta? On the Karakoram Highway? In Kohistan? At night?

Absolutely.

I had slept less than three hours the night before, but I was much too excited to care. I slid in behind the steering wheel on the right-hand side of the vehicle, and the driver stretched out in the back. Left hand on the gears, my American mind struggled to figure out the reverse pattern, and finally wiggled the lever into gear.

I started to pull out of the parking lot slowly, and the driver suddenly sat up. No, that way, that way, he corrected me, pointing. I had reversed the directions along with the gears in my mind and had started to go back toward Rawalpindi. Hmm, I thought, good thing he was still awake.

The next few hours were unforgettable. Yawning caverns of darkness as we rounded each bend, sudden washouts riddled with two-foot-deep potholes that could take out an axle, shadows behind boulders in the moonlight that might hide troops of bandits. Greg Ritchie sat beside me, dozing off and then suddenly waking up and barking out "left" whenever he sensed that I was drifting to the right (wrong) side of the road. By 4:00 a.m., I was starting to see things that weren't there. Tunnels in solid walls of rock, rats scuttling across the road, that kind of thing.

"D'you think we can fit through that tunnel?" I asked Greg anxiously, nodding toward a gaping black hole in the cliff ahead.

"Where? I don't see any tunnel," he answered.

I pulled the van over to the edge of the road. "Your turn to drive," I announced.

Knowing your limits is as important as being able to push them.

I distrust the incommunicable;
it is the source of all violence.

—JEAN-PAUL SARTRE

THE PHONE FACTOR

We caught up with the team. I sensed an indefinable tension as soon as we drove into the customs compound. Only two members of the team, Fred Ziel and Wayne Wallace, stood up to wave to us from the other side of the gate. They had just finished loading the truck with our 155 bags after clearing customs, and Jeff was predictably impatient to get going. Over the next several days, the rest seemed aloof, indifferent to the fact that the phone had been recovered. This didn't offend me; Fred and I had been the only two members of the team who had managed to find significant sponsorship for the expedition, and it was only natural that most of the team wouldn't understand the value of the phone. Still, it was another warning sign.

Oddly enough, over the course of the next three months, the team's attitude toward the phone would be anything but aloof.

"Most of us," Ivan Ramirez reluctantly admitted in a web dispatch in mid-July, "could scarcely imagine being here without the luxury of communication. The sat phone and computer enable us to talk with friends, family, and significant others. It's not hard to identify a team member who has recently heard from friends or family. They smile and seem above all the banter."

When the tensions between team members reduced our conversations to snippy, absurd little digs, or when we were pinned down for three torturous weeks in July by bad weather, the three-meter dome communications tent with the phone and laptop became a gateway to another world, an escape from the monotony and the negativity at Base Camp.

It also became the portal for all of our frustrations, which were magnified through the voices of the two professional journalists and our own team members reporting about each other. "Reporting" is a generous term for what some members of our team were doing in the Internet dispatches. Ranting is more accurate. "Cyber-ranting," Ivan, the emergency doctor, called it. "The computers were the classic drugs," he wrote. "I needed them, but I hated the rhetoric they were facilitating."

Our team wasn't the only team experiencing the deleterious effects of the media. Two of the other teams at Base Camp, a 14-member Chinese Tibetan team and a four-member Spanish-Mexican team, had also arrived with satellite communications equipment. Their plans were actually more elaborate than ours. In addition to sending daily dispatches to websites and e-mailing reports to newspapers in their home countries, they were sending live TV broadcasts from Base Camp.

Having so much media on the mountain affected the climb. When the normal, predictable friction between teams developed over use of the ropes and space for tent platforms at high camps, instead of simply being quietly resolved between leaders, it became a larger-than-life mud-slinging fest aired on the international cyber waves.

"These people [the Spanish-Mexican team] haven't shown any respect," Paul was quoted by one of our team members who happened to be a professional journalist, in the context of a website dispatch about discussions with the Spanish-Mexican team. At Base Camp, the negotiations were being handled, as they should have been, primarily by the two team leaders. This particular team member, however, chose to expand the media coverage to include Paul's opinion. To make the dispatch sound like a fair fight, he included a quote from a member of the opposing side, characterizing Paul's concerns about safety as "pure envy."

Good copy maybe, but not appropriate in the context of an expedition where cooperation and trust are paramount, where any climber's life can suddenly depend on goodwill from others. There is a difference between temporary truths and deeper, lasting realities.

At one point things got so crazy between certain members of the teams, with allegations of theft and other nastiness flying back and forth, that I started to wonder if some external element of the environment wasn't warping people's minds and perceptions. Sure, I had encountered extreme behavior on other expeditions. But nothing quite this universally venomous and extreme. The rocks on the glacier often emitted a strange sulfuric smell when we repitched our tents. Maybe, I thought with a smile, the sulfur had something to do with it.

The phone, I knew, was the real culprit.

FAR WORSE THAN THE CYBER-RANTING WAS THE LACK OF privacy in the e-mails we received via the phone. On the e-mail system that we had been given by our website sponsor, there was no way to put a password on incoming e-mail. The best we could do was have the computer automatically sort the incoming messages into personal folders, and trust each other not to look. As the team friction and media mudslinging started to erode our trust, I think all of us experienced at one point or another the uncomfortable feeling that our e-mails were being read.

In mid-July, one of the handful of climbers I still trusted told me that one of the cameramen was accusing me behind my back of reading his e-mail and, even worse, having e-mailed his wife to let her know that he was having an affair on the expedition. Most of the tensions were like that: a "he said, she said, he said" sort of thing, where everyone was making allegations behind each other's backs and would then retract them when confronted by the individual blamed.

I was both indignant and confused. I would never interfere with someone's private life, especially not a relationship. Not until we were back in the U.S. did I begin to understand the cameraman's reasons. His wife, it turned out, had sent him an e-mail in July asking for a divorce. Her request had nothing to do with his affair, but presumably he had inferred a connection and pegged me as the informant.

At one point I decided to hide my some of own e-mails by using a customize option in the view menu. This wouldn't stop anyone who really wanted to from looking at them, but at least I would know when someone had gone in to my mailbox and switched the settings to "show all messages." My suspicions were confirmed. The settings were switched regularly, sometimes every day.

Instead of causing another team uproar, I simply e-mailed family and friends, explaining the privacy problem and asking them to assume that any messages they sent were being read by the entire team, including journalists. I thought this would be particularly difficult to explain to my daughter, but it turned out to be very easy. She had been reading the fourth Harry Potter book, in which a rancorous reporter named Rita Skeeter is everyone's pest.

"Oh, don't worry about that," she said airily when I started to explain after the expedition, "I know *all* about journalists."

LOOKING BACK ON THE TRIP NOW, THE OBVIOUS QUESTION is whether we could have climbed without the phone—or, more specifically, whether it is possible to procure enough sponsorship for a relatively expensive climb like the North Ridge of K2 without live media coverage. Asking a question like this means also asking a much more fundamental question about how climbers should climb.

The intrepid and inspired H. W. "Bill" Tilman, an avid adventurer and arguably the most famous explorer of the 20th century, once penned a description of the ultimate planning process: "Any worthwhile expedition," he wrote, "can be planned on the back of an envelope."

This quip has become the foundation of an entire grant program, the Gore Shipton Tilman Grants. "Shipton and Tilman," the grant administrators write, "were strong advocates of traveling in small compact teams, staying nimble, unburdened by numbers of porters and excessive tonnage. Selection of the team was paramount; closely knit friends with mutual respect and trust for one another. They loathed bloat and waste, seemingly getting an extra thrill out of getting by on the barest minimum."

Tilman must have been on Jeff Alzner's mind on that day in May 1998 when he hatched his original plans to climb K2. He was sitting in a tent at 14,000 feet on Denali, waiting out bad weather and scribbling on the back of an envelope. It contained return tickets to Talkeetna on K2 Aviation—which Jeff had won at an auction in the American Alpine Club meeting—and both the tickets and the name K2 Aviation must have seemed auspicious. He was with a couple of friends, Wayne Wallace and Steve Davis.

They were a small, close-knit group of friends. Friends who happened to loathe bloat and waste.

They were a compact team. They'd travel unburdened by oxygen tanks and other hefty gear. They'd nimbly hop, camp by camp, up the hardest mountain in the world, leaving unnecessary items—toothbrushes and toilet paper and other bloat and waste—at Base Camp. They'd use 7mm accessory cord instead of real rope. They'd bring ultralight titanium ice screws and single-wall tents for the summit bid. As the ideas flowed, even Tilman's envelope principle seemed attainable.

Jeff's notes on the back of that envelope read:

THINGS WE NEED TO CLIMB THE NORTH SIDE OF K2:

12 strong climbers

2 good cooks

4 porters

5,000 meters [16,000 feet] of rope

1 permit

12 plane tickets

IN THE ENSUING 24 MONTHS BEFORE THE ACTUAL expedition took place, the embryo of an idea in that tent on Denali grew into a gigantic beast. I was asked to join the expedition in August 1999. The beast at that point already weighed in at thirteen: 12 climbers and one Base Camp manager.

Jeff had never led an expedition prior to K2000, and as I guided him through the planning stages, we quickly realized that we would have to raise an estimated $100,000 in three to six months. He asked me to be the sponsorship coordinator, and I reluctantly agreed. After two years of leading expeditions, I wanted to "just join" a team, to climb without those hassles. But the expedition wasn't going to happen without sponsorship, and there was no way Jeff could find sponsors without help.

By the time we embarked on the K2000 trip, the list of sponsors alone wouldn't have fit on the back of an envelope. In fact, we had an entire notebook crammed with inventories, calculations, and the minutiae of tracking supplies and equipment: 600 kilograms of flour. 2,200 eggs. 900 liters of kerosene. 130 kilograms of propane. 40 tents. 200 wands. 10 radios. 225 locks. One lock-picking kit. Eight Balti porters, each carrying 25 kilograms per day up to the midway point for five days. 20 camel drivers, each carrying 35 kilograms per day for four days, at 15 yuan per kilo (approximately $65 per load). 18 team members, each carrying 25 kilograms per day for three days.

What is it that makes contemporary expeditions so different from the Shipton-Tilman experience?

For one, although Shipton and Tilman traveled into the Shaksgam Valley on the north side of K2, they never actually tried to reach the summit of the mountain. The North Ridge of K2 is perhaps the most sustained, demanding route in the Himalaya. The ridge sweeps in a continuous 12,000-foot line from the base of the mountain to the summit, and climbing the route requires approximately 16,000 feet (5,000 meters) of rope. This is more than twice the amount of rope required, for example, for the Abruzzi Ridge on the south side. It would be impossible to carry and fix this kind of quantity in a reasonable time frame without a relatively large team, or several smaller teams working closely together.

The gear is different, too. Shipton and Tilman brought a mound of gear, but climbers don't wear Grandma's hand-knit boiled wool sweater anymore. Our gear is lighter and much more effective at regulating core body temperature. It increases our chances of survival. It is also much more expensive. So part of the planning process for expeditions today is finding sponsors for some of the critical pieces of equipment—dry-loft down suits for the summit bid, crampons with no-stick snow plates, ultra-warm double plastic boots. Sure, we could probably get away without bringing the warmer aveolite liners for the plastic boots, but then again, there are some distinct advantages to having ten healthy toes.

Of course, once you have sponsors for the gear and raw expenses, they'll need media coverage to justify their dollar investment. This is the hang-up. Finding sponsorship today, in my experience, inevitably means bringing some kind of communications equipment. Back when Tilman began exploring the globe, communication was a military term. The dearth of devices like satellite phones, solar panels, and adventure films made it easier to simply say, "See ya. We'll send a newspaper report back via courier in about three months." Our world is accelerating.

If we reluctantly accept that technology is a necessary evil, that leaves one last question: What could we have done to better manage it on the K2000 expedition?

Privacy was probably the most flagrant problem. Although we will never know the extent to which our privacy was violated, I have a feeling that many of the most serious conflicts could have been avoided if our personal e-mails were not available to prying eyes. Expeditions bringing a laptop and satellite phone to the mountains should make sure that they have software that enables each e-mail user to protect his or her personal folder with a password.

Journalistic style is another issue. If there is a website, and many different members will be dispatching to it, are they all going to be reporting with roughly the same voice? The cybercasts of the past five years have exhibited a wide range of styles. Some were PR pieces that would whitewash or glorify anything negative. Others were a series of quick snippets about the team's progress and logistical concerns. Still others, like ours, were half-veiled naked truths. I got the feeling that readers of our team's dispatches were often confused, trying to read between the lines. One day they would get my esoteric dispatch talking about how the weather was preying on our moods, the next they would get our climber-journalist's blow-by-blow account of the rifts between teams, and then the day after that they'd get a peevish missive from a third writer about climbers who were "posers."

Whatever the style is, it should be an approach everyone agrees on in advance. All of the team members should also have access to all of the dispatches, so that they can read what is written, if they want to, before they receive reactions in e-mails from family and friends.

If there is a website, the editorial style and policies of the website can be another issue. At least three of the uproars on our expedition were sparked by misunderstandings between the team and the editors. The first was when a dispatch that another climber wrote and I sent was not posted to the site immediately, and I was accused of "censoring" the report. The second was when an excerpt of a dispatch I wrote with a poetic description of an avalanche was distributed by editors in a mass e-mail under the title "Near Catastrophe," and many members of our team received panicked "are you O.K.?" messages from family and friends. The third was an ongoing quibble sparked by an email from the editor at the end of the expedition about rights to the digital photos.

Probably the most important potential problem—one that we didn't have to deal with, thank God—is the question of what to do if the worst happens, i.e., what happens if a member of the team is missing, seriously injured, or killed? Will the family be notified first? Who has the family contact info, anyhow? (Keep a copy with the sat phone.) If one of the team members is killed, what are the family's wishes? What would that climber have wanted? I have seen several teams grapple with hard questions when it's too late to ask, and I know of a current legal case regarding a death on Everest in which there was some miscommunication between the expedition leader and the family of the climber who died.

THE DEMANDS OF TECHNOLOGY DEFINITELY ADD another dimension to the climbing. But does that mean it's impossible for expeditions to be simple? In my opinion, the Shipton-Tilman principle is as applicable as ever. The Gore grant program's mandate to climb in a group of "close-knit friends with a mutual respect and trust," for example, is timeless. In the month before the K2OOO expedition, I was reminded of how important this advice is on a trip to Bolivia. I was climbing with a group of three good friends; it was a beautiful, successful journey, with absolutely no problems.

Of course, there are a couple of caveats. A century ago, when very little was known about the far-flung regions of the globe, exploration without extensive research and planning was appropriate. Today, the era in which travelers could try a first ascent and be excused for their ignorance is gone. A solid first step in responsible expedition preparation, in my opinion, is visiting the American Alpine Club library in Golden, Colorado, and perusing the exhaustive resources on the Internet. Generate as many envelopes of research as possible. Adventures today are about exploring the unpredictable, not the unknown.

The units have changed, too. Megabytes have replaced envelopes.

"Worthwhile" expeditions are those that can be planned in a single megabyte, those in which every detail is researched and planned.

Planned, but not predictable.

The mountain was in labour, and Jove was
afraid, but it brought forth a mouse.

—Tachos, King of Egypt

MAZAR

At least our K2000 expedition, even if it lacked simplicity, had a solid base of unpredictability. One of the most interesting postexpedition comments was the speculation from one climber, Dr. Fred Ziel, that we might have made the summit if it hadn't been for Mazar.

"You never know," Fred pointed out. "If it hadn't been for the problems at Mazar, we would have made it to Base Camp a week earlier, and we would have had another week of good weather to fix ropes before the storms in July. We would have been in a much better position to push to Camps 3 and 4 when the weather finally broke."

Mazar is a remote Chinese army outpost at 12,000 feet with approximately 300 troops. Near the border of Pakistan and India, it is also near the line of control established in 1972 for the disputed state of Jammu and Kashmir. On our approach to the point along the road where we would rendezvous with our 72 camels (beasts, not cigarettes), we had to go through the Mazar checkpoint.

As we approached the army base via jeep on May 30, it was hard not to feel a sense of foreboding. We were traveling in a convoy of approximately 40 covered trucks, each of which was filled with Chinese troops. We noticed signs of recent heavy garrisons.

There are no villages, no roads other than military roads, no common means of travel through this corner of the globe other than by foot or camel. The troops, hundreds of them, were clearly going into the mountains for either rigorous exercises or activity. What is it about these mountainous regions, I wondered, that makes them such a fierce bone of contention between China, India, and Pakistan? What could there possibly be to defend?

I took a photo of young men hanging out of the truck ahead of us in the convoy, and they smiled and waved. Farther up, after our jeep had tried to pass several more trucks, I tried to take another. The more seasoned troops in that truck frowned and started to gesture severely, indicating that photographs were forbidden. No surprise, I thought glumly, thinking of a previous attempt to get People's Liberation Army to smile and say cheese.

Jeff and I had traveled to Beijing in February, three months prior to the expedition, to organize the logistics of the expedition with officials at the Chinese Mountaineering Association. We had rented bicycles to "train" on our day off. I was determined to get a traffic ticket on the streets of Beijing. It seemed like the perfect souvenir. Speeding, crossing an intersection at the wrong moment, riding a bicycle through Tiananmen Square. Something like that. I did all of these, to no avail. Finally I hopped off my bike with a camera to take a photo of a soldier in front of the gates to the Forbidden City. That almost did it. The guy agreed to let me take his photo if I agreed to give him my film afterward. I made a counter offer: I'd swap two rolls of film for one of his tickets, new or used. Both worth about 800 yuan—a fair trade.

He didn't accept. Maybe I should have offered three rolls. Or perhaps, as a friend who went to Harvard Business School suggested, the problem was a cultural chasm. "Your offer, Heidi," my friend pointed out, "was predicated on an elemental comprehension of the concept of capitalistic gains."

IF THE RESISTANCE TO PHOTOGRAPHY WAS PREDICTABLE, the fact that we had two breakdowns and one accident on the way to Mazar was even more so. The road to Mazar is unpaved and riddled with washouts. Traveling in a convoy of army trucks, we were like gnats in a herd of elephants. One of our seven sport-utility vehicles lost its main suspension pin, and another had a flat tire. Then the SUV carrying Ivan and Shawn collided with a flatbed truck, hitting it just behind the cab, in one of the gas tanks. Although it was wedged under the truck and had to be pulled out by another vehicle, they were miraculously able to roll the remainder of the way to Mazar.

We made the decision to camp at Mazar that night. Camping near an army base, we were told, was strictly forbidden, but the commander, a three-star general, invited us to spend the night in the barracks. Our rowdy group of 18 Americans sleeping on camel-hair mattresses and rice pillows as "guests" at a Chinese Army base? Highly unusual.

The military movements we had witnessed en route to Mazar, we discovered, were "sensitive." No foreigners were allowed in the area for at least another four to five days, perhaps another few weeks. We would have to drive back the way we had come, 140 dirt-road miles, over a 16,000-foot pass and through the Taklamahan Desert, to Yecheng, where we would have to wait until the troop movements were complete.

Nothing, not even a friendly game of basketball with the troops in the garrison, could persuade them that we were not a threat to national security. Of course our team won the game (USA-40, PLA-28), which might have been the single most grievous mistake we made on the expedition. In a similar game at the Pakistan-Chinese border post the week prior (before Greg and I caught up), the team had apparently managed to save more than $3,000 in fees by graciously losing to the Chinese customs officials.

As Fred pointed out at the time, "When in Rome, do as the Romans do. When the region is under martial law and the local Roman with the loaded weapon says go back to Yecheng, one tends to capitulate."

The what-ifs at Mazar were numerous. What if we had come a week or even a day or two earlier? What if we had lost the basketball game? What if that vehicle hadn't been delayed by the collision with the military truck? What if the world was a slightly saner place in which people did not wage wars over a frozen wasteland of rock and snow?

Of course what-ifs are mere rhetoric now, curiosities and landmarks. The labyrinth is like that. The paths you travel are very quickly swallowed in the darkness of the past, and it is difficult to know which doors were dead ends and which were real options. What would have happened if you left one minute later? One day? One year?

On the way back to Yecheng, our liaison officer from the Chinese Mountaineering Association surveyed the caravan of armored tanks rolling in under cover of darkness and grimly wondered whether we'd be able to get permission to enter the Shaksgam region at all. Clearly the CMA had not been privy to the army's plans.

FORTUNATELY, PERMISSION TO PROCEED THROUGH THE Mazar checkpoint was suddenly granted two days later, and we simply turned around and drove back. On the drive, with the anxiety of the bureaucratic delay relieved, certain members of the team began to refocus their abundant negative energy in my direction. Given the possibility that our dispatches to the website could be reviewed by Chinese Army officials in Beijing, we hadn't sent any news in three days. I was anxious to send news as soon as possible, and these team members didn't want me to say anything about the military situation. We had a heated discussion about it at the lunch stop. Apparently they were worried I might write something that could be considered offensive or classified information by Chinese officials.

They needn't have worried. I shared their desire to get out of China without spending any unnecessary time in prison.

My dispatch that night was innocuous:

Mazardala
Sunday, June 4, 2000

Good news! The permission from the military to proceed through the checkpoints at Mazar and Mazardala was suddenly granted late Friday night, and we are now at the "end of the road," waiting for the camels to reassemble so that we can begin the trek tomorrow. The unexpected thaw in military relations was probably due to the assistance provided by Mr. Jim Levy and the military attaché at the American Embassy in Beijing, at the request of Representative James Rogan, Representative Mark Udall, and Senator Ted Kennedy. We are deeply appreciative of their interest and support.

The beginning of the trek is always a period of introspection, a time to think about both the journey ahead and the families and friends we have left behind. We have all been receiving e-mails from home in the past few days, and we know we wouldn't be here without the encouragement of hundreds of friends, spouses, parents, climbing partners, and sponsors.

I, for example, wouldn't have been able to join this expedition without the help of my parents, who are caring for my daughter, Devi. Special thanks go to my very tolerant, supportive mother. She's the only person in the world who can tell whether I have a stuffed-up nose from the way I answer the phone. She's the CEO of a group of child-care centers, has written a book that is in its fifth printing, and bakes killer chocolate chip cookies.

Being the mother of a high-altitude climber is not an enviable position, especially when you consider the bizarre habits climbers cultivate and the inevitable generation gap. I had a hard time just before my first expedition explaining why I was packing a water bottle with a skull-and-crossbones penned on it. (It's my pee bottle.) And I still haven't managed to convince her that pit zips are an excellent way of managing underarm odors.

Probably the most difficult part of being the mother of a climber is receiving news. My letter from today, for example, might read:

Dear Mom,

The Chinese Army finally finished moving all of their tanks and troops, and let us through the checkpoint at Mazar yesterday. The eight-hour off-road jeep ride through Mazar to the end of the road was uneventful, aside from one minor accident—our jeep drove into a ditch at about 30 mph. I hit my head on the windshield, but the headache went away in a couple of hours and neither the jeep nor the windshield were damaged.

Our camel drivers were waiting for us at Ilik, the "end of the road." When I went over to talk to them, one of them pointed first at me and then himself and then the bushes. I politely declined this particular invitation, but agreed to taste the soup they were brewing over an open fire. There were noodles in the soup, and some kind of black meat. They had just added cerebral matter from a goat's head that was being roasted on a stick, so I think the meat was probably goat. Your chicken soup is much better.

We woke up this morning to the sound of prehistoric screams echoing off the canyon walls around us. There are 71 camels here with us, and most of them are not very happy about this little journey. We were supposed to have 75 camels, but 4 of them died on the way here. One got hit by a jeep, another was killed by rockfall, and two more died of altitude sickness. This is the bad news. The good news is that our team was more fortunate than the camels. There are still 18 of us.

Please give Devi kisses and hugs for me tonight and remind her that I want to know what the tooth fairy brought her in her next e-mail. I am missing you all.

Lots of love, Heidi

... to be able to pray we need silence
silence of the heart.
The soul needs time to go away and pray
to use the mouth
to use the eyes
to use the whole body.

—MOTHER TERESA

SILENCE OF THE HEART

All expeditions to the north side of K2 entail camels and river crossings, and even a cursory account of the K2OOO expedition would be incomplete without a mention of the Shaksgam River Valley and the camels. The approach to the north side of K2 crosses the Aghil Pass (15,470 feet; 4,715 meters), and then drops down into the valley of the Shaksgam River (12,470 feet; 3,800 meters), a broad, brown silt plain filled by cold, braided streams that crisscross the alluvium.

Although the valley is filled with water, the altitude and harshness of the rapidly shifting environment combine to make it a desert climate. In spots where the constantly shifting beds of the river have not recently washed everything out, there are small oases of green. These are the only vegetation, the primary source of food for the camels and the fuel for the camel driver's campfires. It is a fragile environment, and heavy expedition traffic would be a problem. Fortunately, it is still relatively undiscovered.

The biggest challenges on the camel section of the approach are the river crossings in the Shaksgam. Because the meandering river swings from one vertical wall of the valley to the other, each day of the trek is approximately 15 miles of scouting out spots where the rivers are not too wide, not too deep, and not too fast.

Fred and I arrived at one oasis after three hours of approximately 20 river crossings, some deep, some shallow, all very cold. Two of our teammates, Ivan and Shawn, were already there.

"You got weeded?" Ivan asked me as we approached, looking at my wet hair and blue face with an incredulous wide-eyed stare. "Did you get dunked?"

I usually reserve the word "weeded" for conversations about gardening, but in this particular context I didn't need any translation. The meaning was clear. I had been making my way across a swift, cold, waist-deep river when suddenly my feet were swept out from under me, and I found myself thrashing and flailing downstream, trying to keep my head above water with a 50-pound pack on my back and trekking poles in my hands.

The Gore-Tex jacket and fleece I was wearing were still soaked when we arrived at the campsite. They were completely useless. As useless, in fact, as Shipton and Tilman's wet wool would have been.

"Righteous," Ivan grinned.

Righteous? My rapidly expanding K2000 vocabulary had just expanded by two more words. We were a truly amazingly diverse team, the 18 of us. Carpenters, students, doctors, writers, chefs. Single, married, engaged, divorced, committed, not so committed. The only things we had in common were our nationality and our passion for K2.

We all spoke English, but somehow we had hugely different vocabularies. And so, to bridge the language and culture gap, we found ourselves developing an expedition vernacular.

"Stickage," for example, was snow that was falling and starting to adhere to a surface. "Check out the stickage up on that ridge."

"Frothage" was white water, haystacks, holes, or any other sort of turbulence that might give an indication of the depth or speed of the river. "I wouldn't try to cross there. Way too much frothage."

"Death holes" were pockets, sinkholes, crevasses, or other aberrations in the otherwise benign fabric of the universe. "White death" was a mayonnaise-based salad, served after being exposed to wildly fluctuating temperatures for four days or more. "Talking to the rocks" was vomiting. The "Shag Zone" was a neighbor-free area around two couples' tents. The "dung putter" was a trekking pole that we used to play golf with camel dung. "Blame-storming" was the process of finding innovative ways to explain who was responsible when those inexplicable mishaps happened. "Teamwork" was a noble term Jeff used when he was having a good day. And so on.

AFTER FIVE DAYS OF TREKKING WITH THE CAMELS, WE finally arrived at a spot at the foot of the Qogiri Glacier that we decided to call the "Camel Dump."

As we flopped our packs down, I sensed a collective frustration. We had been moving through clouds and mist for three days, knowing that we were within sight of K2 without actually being able to see it.

"That water comes from K2," one of the team members commented hopefully, pointing at a river that is gushing from the snout of the glacier.

"D'ya think this rock came from it, too?" someone else asked flippantly, picking up a particularly unattractive, nondescript hunk of granite.

After three weeks of traveling halfway around the globe, we were all feeling dejected that we couldn't even see the mountain.

Then, at 6:10 p.m. Xinjiang time on Sunday, June 11, the veil suddenly lifted. The clouds obscuring the glacier dissipated, and there it was—the upper third of K2, Qogiri, Ch'ogori, the Great Mountain, cold and beautiful and uncompromising, floating above the horizon. With turbulent, windblown mists shrouding the lower part of the vision, it had a surreal aura, and after the initial shouts of surprise, we all simply stood and stared, muttering completely inadequate expressions of awe.

THE FINAL STAGES OF THE APPROACH, CARRYING LOAD AFTER load up the glacier, first to the mid-camp and then up to Base Camp, were an exhausting but meditative process. For the first time since we had left the U.S. four weeks before, I found I had time to myself. Time to think, to look silently at the mountain and then within. It might have been a "strategic" mistake to isolate myself from the team, as one member later suggested, but after nine months of working around the clock, desperately scrounging up sponsorship for the team, and four weeks of traveling with a raucous group of 18, I needed the space. I needed to siphon off all the unnecessary thoughts and emotions, to refocus and find my inner balance before we started to climb.

After several days of trips up and down the glacier, I wrote in my journal:

June 17, 2000

Today is a welcome rest day for me, a respite from the arduous task of ferrying loads from the mid-way point up to Base Camp. I have washed my hair, my socks, and my etcetera; the first warm water bathing session I've had since we left Yecheng some two eons ago.

It was another sky-blue summit day, and I can't resist sitting up on the moraine above camp after my bath, ogling at all of the peaks that line the glacier. There is one with a pure snow dome, a silky line of white etched against the dusty blue sky. Another with striated black-and white summit ridge, folds of granite thrust through the crust of the Earth before the dawn of vision. A third with a double-tooth fang, twin rock pyramids that cap a sheer black face.

"6022, 6014, 6302," the Chinese map in my lap says. Altitudes (in meters) only. No names. Why name a point on the map if you never go there, if no one has ever been there before? Names are a means of possession, of making things a part of our personal realities.

It reminds me of a cartographer I met in the drainage of the Braldu River, on the other side of K2, several years ago. In places of no names, names of places can change, depending on your point of view. "The place where you find water" may be the same as "the place where the ibex come to drink," or "the camp site by the river." The cartographer was frustrated with his Pakistani guides, who were giving him different answers for the same point on the map. "Look at this," he told me, handing me his notebook with visible agitation, "I have recorded four possible spellings for the name Urdukas, all phonetically incompatible. And they say there are three peaks over here," he jabbed a pencil at the map, "that all go by the name of Mount Pata Nahi."

"Mujea pata nahi," I later learned, means "I don't know," in Urdu. "Mount I-don't-know."

Perhaps we should be slightly more tolerant of those climbers two generations ago who chose to simply assign their own names and their own meanings to points on the globe.

Points like Everest, and K2.

Meaning is a matter of perspective; it's a shifting, changing thing.

I passed one of the Balti porters coming down yesterday. We exchanged greetings, and I found myself studying the contours of his face like a landscape—every twist, every wrinkle. It is a face that has led a life shaped by wind and snow and sand, roughened into a texture made more beautiful by strife.

How do we choose what to lose? How do we decide to give up the security of our homes, to live on the edge, where the instruments of time test our strength? This porter is working to support his family. He was carried here, to this part of the world, by invisible forces that sweep his life along like a grain of sand in the river. Maybe he didn't choose to endure this hardship; maybe it simply happened. Our choices are sometimes shaped by the events around us.

Events wither and weather and sometimes forever change us, but we survive. As I looked at the man perched on a rock in front of me, I realized that I have been shaped by the forces of life. The events in my past are part of me, part of each one of us, a part of ourselves that we can't choose to lose.

All I can do is take each new challenge, each difficult day, and hope I weather it as gracefully as the landscape around me.

He who rides a tiger is afraid to dismount.

— PROVERB

SPLITOVAS

After a week's portage, a full five weeks after we had left the U.S., we finally began climbing. This is one of the unique aspects of climbing on the north side of K2; situated in the isolated western regions of China, it is easily the most remote of all the 8,000-meter climbs. It is not the kind of place where you'd want to have an attack of appendicitis. If anything happens during the expedition, helicopter evacuation is unavailable. Even retreat on foot is impossible once the Shaksgam River is in flood. From late June through the end of July, the river is too high even for camels.

Climbing on the north side of K2, I quickly discovered, was different from the Abruzzi Ridge. Unlike the south side, where the route on the lower half of the mountain is relatively sheltered from avalanches and offers solid placements for anchors in the rock, the lower part of the route on the north side is extremely avalanche-prone and entirely on ice and snow. Although climbing on white surfaces is technically easier, it can be more difficult to protect. Anchors on the mountain can be subject to strong forces—wildly variant weather conditions, avalanches, and high winds—that can either melt out the screws or pickets or bury them in so much snow that the slack built in for ease of clipping into the rope is lost.

With a total of 29 days of snow in July alone, our primary problem in 2000 was the instability of the slopes above the route going up to Camp 1. Climbers who had been on the route in other years urged us to wait for at least a day after a storm to allow the excess snow to slough off. The problem was, by the time the reasonable weather came in August, we were so close to our scheduled departure date of August 21 that we didn't have time to allow the slopes to consolidate.

Part of the avalanche problem was that the route up to Camp 2 crosses into an area above the route to Camp 1. If we weren't careful, a simple point release triggered by a climber crossing this slope could escalate into a full-scale avalanche below.

Going "up" to Camp 2 didn't mean just going up. It meant going up and over and up and over and up and over. In order to get to the little platform of snow on the ridge where we situated the camp, we had to traverse around three long fingers of rock that extend down from the ridge. Each traverse was a 100- 200-meter-long session of kicking crampons across 45-50 degree slopes of green ice and rotten nevé. The fastest technique for getting across seemed to be front-pointing with one foot, and "frenching" (using sidepoints) with the other.

Mike had a name for this technique: "pied à splitova," he called it, or just "splitova." Demonstrating splitovas on level ground, splitova right, splitova left, would look like a happy little jig. You could do it with a smile. Up on the route to Camp 2, though, we could only splitova one side. And splitova right, splitova right, splitova right, for hours at a time, didn't even remotely resemble a jig. I, for one, couldn't do it with a smile. By the end of the first hour on each trip up, the little bones and tendons in my right foot were screaming for mercy.

At least the agony of endless splitoving was alleviated by the interest of various landmarks along the way. Just two pitches above Camp 1, for example, there was a door-sized chunk of granite I called "The Portal." Ivan discovered this particular rock on a tenuous sort of lead, with a belayer anchored to only two axes, and a single screw left on his harness. Looking for a solid place to anchor the rope, he pulled on the stone, and discovered that the entire thing moved ever so slightly, with a deep grinding sound, like the entrance to Aladdin's cave. He gently finessed the rock back into place, leaning on it with his body weight, and tied the rope to the snarl of old ropes around another rock behind it.

To "trundle" (knock off) the Portal would be death to climbers below and possibly the grand finale of Camp 1, or the ropes leading up to Camp 1, so we passed some of the idle time in the tents at Camp 1 debating the relative merits of duct tape, rope, and other techniques for sticking it in place.

After the Portal was a string of Mike's anchors. One "V-thread" (a technique for threading a strand of rope through a hole in the ice), one Ushba ice screw, equalized, and one double-overhand loop for clipping in. Neat, predictable, precise. Climbing through this section of the route was a exercise in rhythm; every 50 feet or so, clip, snap, unclip, move on. In his alternate real life, Mike is a carpenter and contractor. I imagined him nailing up a plank with the same automatic precision. As I went through this section I sometimes I imagined that I was a machine of precision, too, using the section to track numbers—heart rate, gain in altitude, rate of ascent, drop in barometric pressure. At each anchor I checked the Suunto altimeter on my wrist: clip, check, snap, unclip.

In the middle of one of the traverses was a field of pockmarks in the snow, from rocks falling off the ridge above. It was just after this field, on the third or fourth ascent to Camp 2, that I dropped one of my carabiners (clip, check, fumble for a drink, drop, oops...), and dumbly watched it sail through 4,000 empty feet of space to the glacier below. The fact that it spun around and around, almost floating as it fell, startled me. Somehow it is easy to forget, when you are living in a vertical world, that you are constantly struggling against the dictates of gravity. The struggle becomes mundane. Seeing a rock fall is analogous to walking down the street and suddenly observing a rock fly up into the sky. It takes a moment for your brain to reorient itself, to figure out why the object went down like that, and why it took so long to reach the bottom.

ASIDE FROM THE MEDITATIVE BENEFITS OF ESTABLISHING a rhythm, there was a reason I kept checking the numbers, particularly the barometric pressure. At sea level, barometric pressure typically hovers around 30 inHg, depending on the weather. On K2, it ranges from approximately 16 inHg at the base of the mountain (16,700 feet; 5,100 meters) to about 10 inHg on the summit (28,250 feet; 8,611 meters), depending on the weather. The weather around

K2 is volatile, and sudden drops in the already low pressure are much more pronounced than barometric changes at lower altitudes. A sudden drop in the pressure can effectively mean a sudden increase in the altitude.

On my first trip up the ropes to Camp 2 in late June, this is precisely what had happened. By the time the group I was climbing with had reached the top of the lines that had already been fixed, the pressure had dropped by a full tenth of a point in less than two hours, to 14.00 inHg. Fred began leading a pitch across the third traverse. Above him were whorls of mist and snow dancing on the ridge and the telltale signs of high winds. And behind, the clouds surging over the Savoia Pass from Pakistan told us what the numbers had already indicated: The weather was disintegrating.

We huddled in the spindrift at the belay stances and fixed ropes for another three hours, and then beat a hasty retreat to Camp 1. The following morning, our tents at Camp 1 were buried in six inches of fresh snow, and we found ourselves watching the soft underbellies of spindrift avalanches hissing like white waterfalls over the lip of our cave. We retreated again, hastily, to Base Camp.

That was July 2. The drop in barometric pressure marked the beginning of a monotonous three weeks of storms. Another four weeks would pass before we made significant progress on the mountain again, and not until August 9 did I find myself in the first group of climbers moving up to sleep at Camp 3.

By that time the rifts among teams had been repaired, and we were climbing in a loose-knit international group of climbers: five members of our expedition, the four members of the Spanish-Mexican team, and two Japanese climbers. We had all pushed up to 24,500 feet (7,500 meters) the week before, and, although it is wise to spend at least one night above 23,000 feet (7,000 meters) and then go all the way back to Base Camp before trying to summit an 8,000-meter peak, I think we were all thinking the same thing: if the weather holds, let's push as high and as fast as possible.

Four hours after leaving Camp 2, one of the Mexican climbers, Hector Ponce de Leon, and I found ourselves in the middle of a snowfield just above two Japanese tents and a recently pitched Chinese camp. It was about 300 feet below the spot where we had stashed our tents the week before, but we were both carrying extra tents for Camp 4. One of the Japanese climbers had given us hot tea as we passed his tent, and the same thought was clearly on both of our minds: There is strength in numbers. Although we had planned to put Camp 3 slightly higher, it seemed to make sense to be within earshot of each other in order to coordinate efforts to fix the final stretch of ropes to Camp 4.

Hector tossed down his pack and started shoveling. When the rest of our team arrived, we all agreed to pitch our tents in the same vicinity, at least temporarily.

If the weather had held, the spot would have been fine—but the summer of 2000 was a statistics-defying season of gnarly weather, and we had no such luck. It started to snow that evening. We all stayed at Camp 3 the next day, snowbound.

I WAS LYING IN MY TENT RESTING AFTER MELTING SNOW ON the stove that hung from the tent poles when the first pile of spindrift hit.

Phhumph. It happened too quickly to think. One moment I was lying in my sleeping bag, the next I was sealed in a neat little envelope of snow, with the tent completely flattened under a mass of snow, and the poles twisted like snakes inside it. Chaos. I pushed up on the tent, tried to make space to breathe, to move. Tried to stay calm, wondered if the other tents had been hit. I squirmed around and found the zipper to the door, unzipped it and tunneled out.

Phhumph. Another load of snow. Quick, find your boots, Heidi, I told myself, but the snow was too heavy and I couldn't move. Greg and another teammate, Jay, had found shovels. I waited while they freed enough of the tent for me to dig out my boots, suit, and crampons.

The tent had been destroyed. Mike and Greg dug another platform in what seemed like a more sheltered section of the slope, and we put up another tent, determined to sleep at Camp 3 for a second night, hoping the weather would clear. Again, no such luck.

At 3:00 a.m., another series of wet, heavy spindrift slides hit the camp. Mike and I had been sleeping with knives on strings around our necks, thinking we might need to cut our way out of the tents. We didn't need the knives, but it was obvious by about 4:00 that we needed to bail, and quick.

Greg rappelled down to the tents below us to make sure that everyone had survived, and we scrambled for a couple of hours, trying to keep the tents unburied long enough to get our equipment out and anchor everything to a rock wall above the camp. By 8:00, we were down at Camp 2, helping other climbers shovel out platforms that had been smothered by snow. By noon we were slurping soup back in Base Camp.

IT WAS WHEN I GOT DOWN TO BASE CAMP AFTER THAT little adventure and was confronted with another wave of hostility that I realized just how unsafe and ridiculous the rifts within our own team had gotten. The vestibule of my tent, I discovered, had been littered with trash while I was up on the mountain. There was a sticky energy gel smeared all over the zipper and the inside walls of the tent—"semen," Paul called it. It looked as though a journal that I had accidentally left in my tent had been thumbed through. Paul had composed and distributed an e-mail about me to everyone on the team, filled with totally inappropriate vulgarity.

I had already accepted the fact that my opinions on the expedition were disregarded by Paul and Gill due, they said, to my "excessive, female way of putting things."

I had accepted the fact that they and others would play childish pranks to discourage me from climbing. Filling my boots with snow, "borrowing" my ice axes.

I had accepted the fact that they couldn't seem to talk directly to me or use my name. "That c...," was the accepted appellation.

I had even accepted the fact that other members of the expedition felt trapped, unable or unwilling to do anything to stop the abuse. "We were held mentally hostage by two individuals for four months," one member commented after the expedition.

But for some reason the vulgarity of the stickiness on my zipper, and the blatant violation of the privacy of my tent bothered me more than anything else. Why is it, I wondered, that a woman has no protection on a mountain, simply because she is outside her home country? Although Paul and Gill's behavior was extreme, I know I am not the first female climber to experience inappropriate behavior and remarks. I felt alone and vulnerable. I didn't mind the alone part; I am used to that. It was the vulnerability that bothered me.

On a deeper, more interesting level, I find myself wondering how the situation with the rest of the team disintegrated to the point where everyone was unable or unwilling to defend me.

Despite the factions and disagreements, the expedition would never have happened except through a phenomenal collective will. It was a dream we all agreed to dream; our ambition to climb K2 was a mass fantasy, shared in varying degrees by team members, friends, mentors, family, and sponsors. It was a hope, an aspiration, an against-all-odds dare to believe in the barely possible.

So why, given the strength of the beginning, did we find ourselves bickering? Eighteen mature adults—doctors and teachers and carpenters—alone on a glacier, a month away from the nearest jeep or Coca-Cola, arguing about who said and who gets and who thinks what.

It wasn't just the weather. The three weeks of snow exacerbated the problem, but it wasn't the cause.

It wasn't just the phone. The phone just gave us an audience and an outlet.

It wasn't just the fact that I didn't have one of Wanda's guardian angels, a male friend or husband to stabilize the gender tensions. This would have helped me, but then the derision would have been directed at someone else.

Maybe it was the sheer force of the dream. It was an ambition that had to be sustained, a hope that periodically needed the sanctification and renewal provided by the rituals of argument and assertion.

Or maybe it was some deeper human need to create a familiar, manageable problem in the world around us. Even as adults, we can't explain all the truly terrifying things in the world, so we sometimes search for the worrisome things that are closer to us and become obsessed with them, peeling off layer after layer of reality until only the pit is left.

AT POINTS IN YOUR LIFE, EVERYTHING YOU BELIEVE IS sucked down into a deep dark hole, and you experience a crisis of faith, an inability to choose, a juncture in the labyrinth in which there is a void of emotions. Life seems irrational, random, futile.

But a new kind of awareness arises from the depths of that emptiness.

New passions and intuitions, new ways of knowing, are born.

You learn to listen to them, and you no longer crave comfort from anyone else.

"He drew men towards him by what was best in them." "It is the gift of the great," she went on, and the sound of her low voice seemed to have the accompaniment of all other sounds, full of mystery, desolation, and sorrow, I had ever heard—...the whisper of a voice speaking from beyond the threshold of an eternal darkness.

— JOSEPH CONRAD,

Heart of Darkness

THE POSTCARD, REVISITED

There. I think that does it. I think the duffel bag of memories has been emptied now. Even the objects that are no longer there have been released. Zee's equipment, Iñaki's xi stone. The hat, too. It is time to send that back now.

THE POSTCARD THAT SAID "DLA WANDA" ON THE BACK IS ALSO gone. "For Wanda," I have been told it meant, in Polish.

What nook or cranny of the globe is it tucked into now, I can't help but wonder? Where did it come from? Who gave it to Wanda?

After I found it in that bookshop, I took it to Base Camp on Kanchenjunga. But returning from Kanchenjunga, I traveled ahead of my bags, and the postcard was lost with them. It was lost en route, probably in the United Arab Emirates, the shipping agent explained. The idea of a bag full of ice axes and down sleeping bags being of any use to a customs agent in Dubai struck me as odd, but I didn't question it. And then, two years later, on the way to Everest, the staff at the Hotel Thamel in Kathmandu produced the bags out of their storage room. Somehow they had been shuffled back into the storage area instead of the airport. I studied the postcard for one longing, fleeting moment again, before packing it back in a barrel with the other Kanchenjunga equipment and leaving it in Kathmandu.

When we came back from Everest, the Kanchenjunga bags were mysteriously missing, again. It seemed even more improbable than ice axes in Dubai. Lightning doesn't usually strike twice. I was miffed.

Now, looking at the whole story, it just seems like a natural part of the way of things.

MAURICE HERZOG, IN HIS TIMELESS ACCOUNT OF THE first ascent of an 8,000-meter peak, invoked the word *freedom*. From the hospital in Paris where he was recovering from frostbite, he wrote, "In my worst moments of anguish I seemed to discover the deep significance of existence of which till then I had been unaware. I saw that it was better to be true than to be strong. The marks of the ordeal are apparent on my body. I was saved and I had won my freedom. This freedom, which I shall never lose, has given me the assurance and serenity of a man who has fulfilled himself. It has given me the rare joy of loving that which I used to despise."

Following his passions, Herzog discovered the freedom of fate. He was able to find a way out of the labyrinth.

IN THE MAZE OF OPPORTUNITIES AND CHOICES AND DEAD ends the labryinth sets for us, it is easy to forget that there is darkness in the world—the kind of concentrated energy that is found in dangerous places, people, and things.

Ananku, the hitchhiker called it. From darkness light is born, the monk said.

Staring at the image of that postcard in my mind, thinking about the dark and twitching shape lurking in the recesses of the darkness, the feeling that there was something almost sinister about it, I know that it is a story that will never be fully told.

There was that moon hanging in the background, the force that lures some climbers to the mountain like moths to a light. There is no point in suppressing these instinctive urges. To do so is to destroy the spirit.

There was that lone tree, branching and forking like a multitude of opportunities, a labyrinth of choices. There was that tiger holding the end of the leash, like a vestige of something wild and feral. The hitchhiker helped me understand this little secret. Those stripes in his skin were ripples, waves of light and dark that disturb reflections in placid surfaces.

There was that naked woman sitting at the base of the tree with the yellow collar. Ah, Wanda—the tiger at the end of your leash was your spirit, your untamable passion for the mountains that captured and sometimes enslaved you. Your reality has intersected with mine, guided me in moments of doubt. I hope I have somehow returned the favor.

POSTSCRIPT

Dear Devi,

It is Christmas Eve. You are curled up in your bed, asleep, breathing in air in big rumbling gasps. I love to watch you like this.

Tomorrow is the day we celebrate the birth of Christ. The birth of love and of forgiveness.

There will be some wonderful gifts under the tree.

There will also be one gift that I cannot put under the tree.

I am giving you a gift that I cannot wrap. I am giving you the gift of putting my passion for K2 in a Pandora's box that I will not open again for as long as I can possibly resist its lure.

There was a time, once, when I thought I would climb forever. Or at least for the rest of this life. After I reached the summit of Gasherbrum, I saw the world from a bird's point of view. Everything was possible.

Possible means something different to me now.

As I stand here quietly watching you not so quietly sleeping, I hope for so much for you. For simplicity. For friendship and integrity.

For the wisdom to accept your failures.

Some people have suggested that I shouldn't climb as a mother. But when will I stop being your mother?

As a mother, I am afraid for you. But of course it is a mother's prerogative, maybe even a mother's duty, to be afraid. Learn to laugh at my fears.

I have learned to laugh at them. Most of them, anyhow.

Now it is time for me to learn to love, and to forgive.

ACKNOWLEDGMENTS

The expeditions described in this book would have been impossible without the support of an amazing multitude of people.

My thanks to all of these people, particularly my parents Nan Lee and Stuart Howkins, who have provided a home and extended family for my daughter and me for the past three years, and who made the journeys I describe possible through endless emotional and intellectual support.

To all of the people of the National Geographic Society, without whose generous financial support and encouragement the expeditions to K2 and Everest would have been difficult, if not impossible.

To the Editor-in-Chief at National Geographic Books, Kevin Mulroy, without whose vision and faith in my abilities this book would never have come to fruition.

To editor John Paine, whose artistry helped give the book substance and form.

To Bill Von Novak, who could have written this book for me.

To Brad Wetzler, for offering sound advice and a balanced perspective.

To Greg Mortenson and Cherie Bremer-Kamp for providing invaluable insight on the cultures and religious nuances of the peoples of the Karakoram and Kanchenjunga Himal.

To Chris Binggeli and Iñaki Ochoa for editing the final version and for keeping me honest.

To Eric Zittel and Glenn Clinkenbeard for their support during an incredibly difficult period.

And to all of the sponsors without whom the dreams and journeys described in this book would never have happened:

Corporate Sponsors
American Nutriceuticals
Bausch & Lomb
Goodman & Mizrac CPA
Novartis Pharmaceuticals
Pakistani International Airlines (PIA)
Priceline.com
The Mazamas
The White Mountain School

Media Sponsors
Greatoutdoors.com
Mountainzone.com
National Geographic TV
The American Alpine Club

Equipment Sponsors

Aloe Up	New England Overshoes (NEOS)
Ambler Mountain Works	Outdoor Research (OR)
Backpacker's Pantry	Pelican Products
Bolle	Pentax
Cascade Designs	Petzl America
Commercial Satellite Systems (CSSI), Inc.	Pigeon Mountain Industries (PMI)
Dana Designs	Power Bar
Eagle Creek	Pur
Forty Below	Rexall/Ultimate Products
Fox River	Solarcraft, Inc.
Gregory Mountain Products	Suunto USA
Institute for Sports Vision	Tillamook Creamery
LEKI USA	Ultimate Directions
Life-Link International	Ushba
Malden Mills (Polartec)	TEVA
Mammut	Yaesu
Montrail	
Mountain Hardwear	

These sponsors are of course all collections of people, of individuals who have shaped my life, as mentors, as facilitators, as climbing partners and creative artists.

Special thanks to David Royle, Michael Rosenfeld, and David Hamlin of National Geographic TV, Jeff Beckham of Greatoutdoors.com (now part of Altrec.com), Margaret Foster, Peter Potterfield of Mountainzone.com, Menno Van Wyk of Montrail, Teresa L'Esperance and Jennifer Miller of Mountain Hardwear, Rick Ridgeway of Adventure Photo, Andrea Gabbard of Miller Freeman, Ruth Ann Brown and Jeff Bowman of Polartec, Manuel Lugli of Focus Expeditions, Chris Speak of Eagle Creek, Kevin Conlin of Solarcraft, Kevin Caccamise of CSSI, Jenni Dow of Fox River, Wendy Smith of Power Bar, Jeff Blumenfeld of Expedition News, Joel Attaway of Forty Below, Bob Sanders of Rexall, Hilary Maitland and Jim Frush of the American Alpine Club, Mark Vermeal of The White Mountain School, Rick Wilcox of IME, Bill Coury of American Nutriceuticals, and Fred Edmunds of Bausch & Lomb, for their continued interest and encouragement.

And, finally, thanks to all of my friends in Pakistan and Nepal.